WHEN YOU'RE FROM BROOKLYN, EVERYTHING ELSE IS TOKYO

Also by Larry King

LARRY KING (*with Emily Yoffe*)
TELL IT TO THE KING (*with Peter Occhiogrosso*)
MR. KING, YOU'RE HAVING A HEART ATTACK
  (*with B. D. Colen*)
TELL ME MORE (*with Peter Occhiogrosso*)

WHEN YOU'RE FROM BROOKLYN, EVERYTHING ELSE IS TOKYO

LARRY KING
WITH MARTY APPEL

Little, Brown and Company
Boston   Toronto   London

First Edition

Library of Congress Cataloging-in-Publication Data

King, Larry, 1933–
    When you're from Brooklyn, everything else is Tokyo / Larry King with
Marty Appel. — 1st ed.
        p.   cm.
    ISBN 0-316-49356-2
    1. Brooklyn (New York, N.Y.) — Social life and customs.   2. New
York (N.Y.) — Social life and customs.   3. King, Larry, 1933–   —
Childhood and youth.   4. Broadcasters — United States — Biography.
I. Appel, Martin.   II. Title.
F129.B7K4   1992
974.7'23 — dc20   92-13453

10   9   8   7   6   5   4   3   2   1

RRD-VA

*Published simultaneously in Canada
by Little, Brown & Company (Canada) Limited*

Printed in the United States of America

To the memory of my mom and dad, Jennie and Eddie Zeiger, and to my dear brother Marty

L. K.

For Irving and Celia Appel, formerly of St. John's Place

M. A.

CONTENTS

ACKNOWLEDGMENTS

OUR THANKS to the following for sharing time and memories: Marty Zeiger, Ellen David, Herb Cohen, Lenny Lefkowitz, Sid Young, Judy Thomas, Irving Appel, Celia Appel, Pat Edwards, Betty Power, the many celebrated graduates of Brooklyn who related their favorite tales, and Little, Brown vice president and executive editor Fredrica Friedman.

WHEN YOU'RE FROM BROOKLYN, EVERYTHING ELSE IS TOKYO

ONE

THOUGHTS
GO BACK

I NEVER FELT AS ALIVE as a broadcaster as during the incredible events of 1991, first during the Persian Gulf war, and then during the failed coup in Moscow, followed by the dissolution of the Soviet Union. Because our CNN signal was up there on the satellite for all to see, we had become the eyes and ears of the world. The CNN correspondents and crews, no doubt feeling the same rush of adrenaline I was feeling, knew that their reports were being seen not only by millions of Americans but also by people around the world, including the political and military leaders of the nations directly affected.

It was one thing to file a report and know that the Pentagon and the State Department had sets on and were listening. It was something else again to know that Saddam Hussein was watching, and that one's very words might influence his thinking, might provoke an action for better or worse.

Nearly every one of our "Larry King Live" broadcasts on CNN during the weeks of the Gulf War was devoted to the

Middle East crisis. Had the war gone on for six, nine, or twelve months, I'm not sure we would have maintained that frenzy, but as it thankfully went by so quickly, the excitement never waned.

Likewise, my radio program on the Mutual Broadcasting System dealt almost exclusively with war news. On the "Larry King Show," we go for two hours and are able to handle more phone calls from around the nation. You get a little more of a grass roots feeling from small-town America. It is a wonderful, democratic exercise. There was nothing like this during the war of my youth, World War II. There was little public dialogue, little forum for it. It was the talk of the streets, but the nation could not engage in a collective dialogue. Radio presented news and some commentary, but not a lot of dialogue. There was no call-in programming. You were influenced by your immediate circle of family and friends.

In the aftermath of the Gulf war, as the nation began to plan its various celebrations of our quick and relatively pain-less victory, we had many calls on both programs from people simply basking in our nation's might, courage, and determination. Early opponents were forced to step to the rear and allow the nation to puff up its chest and flex its muscles. It had been a long time since this level of patrio-tism had swept across the USA.

One night on Mutual Radio, a caller began by saying, "Larry, I'm from Brooklyn, New York, and I just wanted to say . . ."

I don't remember what she wanted to say. We don't really get that many calls from Brooklyn, home of my birth. I have the feeling that those heated political dialogues we used to have on our corner have passed away, a part of another time. True, the dialogues were not very argumentative. We

were all liberal Democrats. We heard a rumor that someone's parents voted for Dewey in 1948, but it was never
confirmed. No, we didn't really debate things, because we
all tended to agree with each other. But we talked a lot
about world events, and sometimes we'd argue them just for
the sake of argument.

I had this impression today that our successors on the
corner didn't care much about politics at all, unless it was
racial politics, the kind that put Bensonhurst and Crown
Heights in the news in recent years. But the fact was, I just
didn't get many calls from Brooklyn. When I got one, it
sometimes jarred me back in time.

Suddenly I could hear the horns blaring from those fat
black automobiles of the 1940s. Everywhere horns blaring.
I was twelve years old. Oh, what excitement in the air! It was
V-E Day, victory in Europe, May 8, 1945. You know that
famous *Life* magazine photo by Alfred Eisenstaedt of the
sailor kissing the girl in Times Square? This was happening
all over New York, a thousandfold. People were hugging
strangers, singing songs, dancing in the streets.

No news today would evoke those kinds of reactions.
None. It's partly because we've lost our innocence. Having
lived through atomic bombs, assassinations, moon landings,
oil embargoes, Korea, Vietnam, Iraq, hostage crises, the fall
of communism, and countless other events from the comfort of our living rooms, enthusiasm and amazement can
never be as high as they were when World War II ended.

In addition, people have placed a reserve upon themselves. Guys would never gather on the corner and sing. I
remember standing there with Herbie and Hoo-ha and Ben
the Worrier and ringing out choruses of " '... when the
führer says, we are the master race, heil, ththth, heil, ththth,
right in the führer's face.' "

Hugging strangers? Forget about it today. You'd be up on a sexual harassment charge before a Senate confirmation hearing some day.

You see this new reserve in baseball. It used to be a ritual: you'd win a World Series game, and you'd pose for a picture in the clubhouse, three or four players, kissing the hero's cheek, mussing the guy's hair for the still photos and newsreel cameras. Do that today and the *National Enquirer* tells you they've all tested HIV-positive.

So we had the freedom of abandon in 1945 which we may never see again. There was such enormous happiness, such a glow of optimism.

It was somewhat more subdued in our Bensonhurst apartment. We were still feeling the loss of my father, who had died suddenly the year before. He was a great patriot, and my mother's joy on V-E Day was tempered with a sigh, and a mild "If your father could have only lived to see this."

The caller from Brooklyn was droning on. Twenty seconds is a long time in radio without making your point. I was snapped back to the present and gave her a "What's your question, Brooklyn?" But my head was still in the forties.

It was a few years after V-E Day. I had a job in the mailroom for Associated Merchandising Corporation. It was an association of smaller department stores, like Burdine's and Jordan Marsh, which could carry more clout by consolidating their buying. That was what Associated did.

The beautiful thing about this job was that they were on the third floor at 1440 Broadway, near Times Square. That was a magical address to me. It was the home of WOR Radio. I loved WOR. Bob and Ray. Arlene Francis. John Gambling. I used to write in for anything they were offering. Even the nameless staff announcers were celebrities to me. I'd ride the elevator up to the twenty-second floor, wait at the top, and then ride down. Sometimes a man would get on and I'd hope he'd speak so I could tell if he was one of the announcers I'd hear doing commercials or station breaks. And the building made me feel like I was an announcer. I'd fantasize about it. I'd walk out of the building and assume that people on the street figured me as an announcer because I was coming out of 1440. I'd stand a little straighter and walk with a little more confidence, for surely, this is the type of posture that would go with those deep, assuring voices.

Later on, when I first started to work for Mutual, WOR was their New York station, before we switched to WNEW. And two or three times a year, we would go to New York and do our broadcast from 1440 Broadway. And I'd go in and get on that same elevator. Associated Merchandising was still on the third floor. And I'd say to myself, "My God, can you believe this?"

"What's your point, Brooklyn?"

"Larry, I just wanted to know when you're having Saddam Hussein on again?"

Amazing.

"Movietone News" was the television of its day during World War II. These were the newsreels, ever optimistic, always patriotic, never giving way to thought-provoking debate. But oh, did we love the newsreels. There was one theater, near Radio City, that only played newsreels. They'd give you the longer versions of the stories you'd see briefly in movie theaters. It was sort of the CNN of its time, while the movie theaters were more like CNN "Headline News."

Great stuff, the newsreels. We'd sit through them twice. There was always a beauty pageant. And spring training. The "Movietone News" cameras loved the Washington Senators in spring training.

"They may have finished seventh last season, but hope springs eternal for Ossie Bluege's Washington Senators, led by the speedy George Case, shown here practicing his sliding."

Then all the players would run toward the camera, pretending to block the lens with their gloves as they went by.

War news was always dramatic. If there was a touch of trouble — "Enemy troops have crossed the border . . ." — there was always a shot of Eisenhower or Patton exhorting their men, or the calming, assuring voice of President Roosevelt.

What a voice.

Roosevelt took office the year I was born and was the only President I knew until I was twelve. He could do no wrong. The newsreels made sure of that.

"AMERICA. THE MARCH OF TIME." There would be the booming voices of Ed Herlihy or Ed Torgeson or the great Lowell Thomas. "But at the White House, all was calm, as President Roosevelt prepared to address the nation."

Driving home from the studio that night, I couldn't help but think about those larger-than-life figures of World War II, and how the war would have played out under today's American television.

"Good evening, ladies and gentlemen. Welcome to 'Larry King Live.' August, 1939. Today, the Germans marched into Poland. Now, here's Larry."

"Thanks very much. Good evening, our guest is Adolf Hitler. Uh, Mr. Chancellor, you were with us a month ago, and you said . . ."

"Nice to see you, Larry, and hello to all your viewers. Love your show."

"When you were with us a month ago, you said you had no plans, no designs beyond the Sudetenland."

"Ve still don't, Larry. No designs. It vas the people of Poland who called for us. The free people of Poland who vished us to take them away from their oppressors. Here, let me show you zis map."

He'd have a map, and he'd describe how his army had moved ahead, answering the cries from the poor Polish citizens, and how he wanted American support, he wanted Americans to understand him.

"You're a vunderful people, Larry. Ve're a vunderful people. Ve should be allies in these difficult times."

"Mr. Chancellor, what about the Jews? We hear stories that . . ."

"Ze Jews, ze Jews, this is an entirely different matter, Larry, somezing ve're taking up in council, there's lots of deals, lots of considerations . . ."

"Albuquerque, New Mexico, you're on with Adolf Hitler."

"Mr. Hitler, you're quite a guy. I think the press has been way out of line with their criticism, and I just want you to know that out here in New Mexico, we think you're doing a great job."

"Sank you very much. I alvays vanted to visit Albuquerque, by ze vay. Hope I have a chance some day."

Visit? He would have toured. People would have sold satin jackets with "1937 Hitler World Tour" on the back. With a logo. He'd have gone on all the shows. His propaganda minister, Joseph Goebbels, would have prepared him.

"Listen, mine führer, the big military films vit the hundreds of thousands of soldiers and the arm vaving and the imploring fists — it vorks vell in our theaters. But the Americans, zay need a folksier style. Look at this snapshot of Vill Rodgers vit the cowboy hat and ze rope. Zis is zeir kind of guy. When you're on Donahue, don't sit so straight in the chair. Cross your legs, laugh a little, don't salute back if someone in ze audience gives you a 'Sieg Heil.' Donahue, Oprah, Sally Jessy, Joan, Geraldo, zese shows are zindicated, zay play in ze mornings and ze afternoons, mostly housevifes in aprons watching, making some strudel for dinner. You hafta appeal to zeir motherly instincts. Ve don't want a var. Ve vant everyone to be happy."

Hitler would make his tour of the talk shows in November. It might have worked. Saddam was terrible on TV. A disaster. Hitler? Might have pulled it off. November was an important time for him to be home, but November was sweeps month in the U.S., and all the producers insisted it would be a waste of everyone's time to come in December. January, forget it, all the ad budgets are gone from holiday spending. Hardly worth it. Maybe in January they'd take Hess or Göring.

"This is 'Nightline,' with Ted Koppel." *Da DA da da.*

"Tonight on 'Nightline,' General Hideki Tojo, now the Premier of Japan.

"Mr. Tojo, for God's sake, Pearl Harbor, what were you thinking?"

"Wait a minute, Ted, wait a minute, there were provocations . . ."

"Monday on 'Sally Jessy Raphael,' what do nymphomaniacs do while all the men are off at war?"

"Tonight on 'Hard Copy,' why did Patton slap that soldier? Why didn't he punch him? The truth behind General George Patton's rise to the top despite those recurring rumors."

"On the next 'Oprah Winfrey,' mistresses of our generals."

                    *   *   *

"Thursday on 'A Current Affair,' the first home videos of Hitler and Eva Braun."

"Tomorrow night on 'Inside Edition,' who is Lucy Mercer, and why do we see her at Warm Springs, Georgia, whenever President Roosevelt vacations there?"

"On 'Now It Can Be Told' tomorrow, exactly what are those concentration camps really about? Geraldo Rivera enters one and discovers instruments of death."

"On the next 'Joan Rivers,' Mr. Blackwell looks at Mrs. Roosevelt's wardrobe and offers the First Lady some fashion tips for a satisfying makeover."

"This is Bryant Gumbel on the beach in Normandy. All this week the 'Today' show will be here in anticipation of the secret American landing expected sometime next week. NBC News has learned exclusively from a War Department source that this is the site of the historic invasion. Willard, how's the weather look for a landing at Omaha Beach?"

" 'The Barbara Walters Special.' Tonight, Franklin Delano Roosevelt.

"Mr. President, I hope you don't mind my asking this, but it has been mentioned, and people are understandably curious — are you in fact a cripple? We never see you stand."

"Next week on 'Prime Time Live,' Sam Donaldson takes us to a Japanese internment camp in California and asks, 'Is this what America is all about?' "

*   *   *

Field Marshal Rommel would have been big. Gigantic. Great general, looked the part, just a soldier, not involved with the nastiness of the camps. There would have been posters, sweatshirts, fan clubs. Dan Rather would walk the sands in Africa with him.

Our generals might not have come off so well. Norman Schwarzkopf was great, but he was off and on in a few months. No time for his image to falter. Eisenhower would have had to suffer through four years of intense news coverage and a public losing patience, anxious to resume normal lives. Ike could have only gone so far on that grin. Peter Jennings and Tom Brokaw would have sliced right through that and gotten to his political ambitions. The public wouldn't have bought the smile when he said he wasn't running for anything; he wasn't even registered with a political party. They would know he was maneuvering. But for what?

Harry Truman could never have made it in '48. Johnny Carson would have done so many Truman jokes by then that he'd be laughed out of Washington.

I pulled into the garage of my apartment building in Arlington, overlooking beautiful downtown Washington and the magnificent Iwo Jima Memorial statue, which was cast in Brooklyn. Just a three-minute drive away stood the Watergate apartments. The building that took down a presidency.
    Herb Cohen has a place there. He's my best friend. Herbie Cohen, adviser to the government, author, lecturer, investor, self-made success. Fellow member of the Warriors. No matter where we live or travel, there is an unbroken bond between us that forever ties us to our roots, to the

borough of Brooklyn. A borough that gave us the feeling that this was the way western civilization in the mid-twentieth century was supposed to live. And it felt so right. There were no driving outside influences telling us otherwise. And here we were, so many years later, so many adventures later, holding apartments within walking distance in the nation's capital.

We had both come so far since the days in Bensonhurst when we lived around the block from each other, when he'd get me in jams and then get me out of them. Brooklyn was to be forever in us. No one who lived in that great borough of Kings County in the 1930s, '40s, and '50s could ever leave without carrying the soul of the streets, the sense of fraternity and friendship, the love of friends, as though they were family. The food was a religious experience. The architecture, a word we never even considered, was unique unto itself. There was concrete and grass and before there were suburbs, this was the perfect blend of a little town in a big city. We breathed it, touched it, and embraced it. From the *whoosh* of a broom handle swing past a Spaldeen rubber ball to the incredible need to drink a chocolate egg cream without long pauses between slurps, these were things that Herbie understood.

To Norman Mailer, a resident of Brooklyn Heights, Brooklyn is "the most real place I've ever been in my life. I love to see the New York skyline from the Brooklyn side. You know all those postcards with the scenic view of Manhattan? They're all shot from Brooklyn. And you know why? Because the photographers want an excuse to be in Brooklyn."

Queens has all of these different communities, and they all have their own mailing address: Flushing, Forest Hills, Rego Park, Woodside, Kew Gardens. Brooklyn has all its own neighborhoods, too — Bensonhurst, Flatbush, Williams-burg, Brighton Beach, Bay Ridge — but we all had the same mailing address, Brooklyn, N.Y. I have a great sense of neighborhood. I haven't lived there in some thirty-five years, but I have a much greater sense of belonging there than I did in Miami or in Washington. I still feel I belong there; that if I were to wake up tomorrow and all that I had accomplished was gone, there would be a place for me somewhere in Brooklyn. It has to do with the love we all had for each other then, not just within the family, but among friends. We all seemed to have marvelous parents, and we all seemed to care for each other. Our parents had brought with them the European experience, along with the monumental decision to move to America. And while we were Americanized, we were acquiring solid, century-old traits from the "old country" that bonded Jews and Italians into a respect for family values that we felt all around us. That's why running into a friend from the neighborhood today is not just a happy coincidence, but a renewal of that unspoken pledge that, somehow, we would always be in touch, we would always be there for each other. We'd argue and fight and then make up and play another day. We had a sense of the larger things in life that meant so much. We were kids, but we had a maturity when it came to relationships. When families huddled their children close together during the mob scenes at Ellis Island so that no one would get separated, a value was transferred to the new world that grew into daily norms in Brooklyn.

Yeah, we talked funny, but we understood each other. And on the streets of Brooklyn, we learned to tackle life and gain respect if we wanted to achieve. It's no surprise that many successful people in all walks of life came off those Brooklyn streets. Brooklyn taught survival, not in a mortality sense, but in a speak-up-for-what-you-want sense. You didn't get far by being shy in that town.

We were familiar with each other, familiar with our surroundings, and knew the code words for competing. Send any of us fifty miles out of town and we might as well be in Tokyo.

I suppose on some public buildings like borough hall or the court house must have appeared the words "Kings County." A perfect complement for Queens County. But we didn't know from Kings. To us it was Brooklyn and will always be Brooklyn, a very special place where Manhattan was "the city," where the egg creams were stirred just so, and where stickball and punchball and marbles occupied the downtime between trips to Ebbets Field. It's my home. All right, I can't resist the obvious. It's King's County, after all.

Hey, Herbie, can you hear me over there in your fancy Watergate? It's me, Zeke, up here on the eighth-floor terrace. Ross Perot was on my show last night. He decided, right there on the show, to consider running for President! William Buckley called it one of the most momentous nights in political history.

We've come a long way from the general program at Lafayette High, my friend.

TWO

EAST NEW YORK

MY FATHER, Edward Aaron Zeiger, was born in Russia in 1900. His town, I believe, was Pinsk, which was not far from the birthplace of my mother, the larger city of Minsk. Dr. Seuss would have had a lot of fun with that. I remember a photo of my father, cracked and fading, but a photo which survived the trip to the United States in 1920. It was of him in the uniform of the Russian army. There were braids on the uniform, indicating, I suppose, a rank of some importance, although his duty would have come as a teenager during the revolution.

He fought in the war that brought communism to Russia, the most significant political development of the twentieth century, for it was a type of government untried in the annals of man until this time. But it failed to survive the century, at least in Russia. It was apparently destined to be a mere phenomenon of the 1900s. I was broadcasting news of its demise when Edward Zeiger would have been ninety-one. He was there for the beginning, and in a sense, I was there at the end. He would have found a satisfaction in that, as though somehow together we had spanned a monumental world event.

His journey through Ellis Island eventually took him to Brooklyn, where he became a boarder in the apartment building in which his future wife, Jennie Gitlitz, resided. They were the same age, but she had come at the age of nine, and was thus in her eleventh year in New York. He learned English quickly, but his accent was more pronounced. She had few memories of Russia, and spoke with only the slightest of accents.

She did remember the passage through Ellis Island and the fear that they would be turned back if they failed their eye examination. That was the big concern, the eye test. Once they cleared that hurdle, they felt they would be home free. There was a disease, perhaps no more than pinkeye, which was reason for nonadmittance, but the fear was genuine, and the relief must have been enormous.

Edward Aaron Zeiger quickly assimilated and became Eddie. He was short, squat, but strong-looking, carrying a build like James Cagney or Jimmy Hoffa. His hair was dark, and would thin but not gray. He wore it back so that it formed a V over his brow, somewhat like Jack Nicholson. His face bore a resemblance to the very handsome actor Dane Clark. (I've met Dane Clark and told him this.) He was, as the Yiddish expression describes it, a *tummler,* a gregarious, outgoing fellow full of stories and laughter and good fellowship. He learned to like American sports like baseball and horse racing.

My parents married when they were twenty-five, and Eddie went into a business he was well suited for. He opened a bar and grill called "Eddie's." It was a little neighborhood joint under the el at 1925 Fulton Street, just a couple of blocks from the walk-up apartment they rented at 208 Howard Avenue. The opportunity to have his own place, something to bear his own name, was what took him from the Lower East Side of New York to Brooklyn. He could be somebody there, and when he found a bar for sale, he grabbed it and moved. While the saloon never made him rich, it provided him with a decent living. He worked there six days a week, and the cops on the beat became his friends and, off duty, his customers. His relationship with New York's finest was such that when I was a tot, my mother made me a miniature police uniform, augmented by a badge with my name, and a little nightstick.

Howard Avenue covered Crown Heights and East New York, which was our neighborhood. Atlantic Avenue and Fulton Street cut these modest streets apart, with East New York forming the northern sector. Howard Avenue ran parallel and in between Ralph Avenue and Saratoga Avenue, with McDougal and Sumpter Streets forming the perpendiculars. One block was about all I could handle in my early years. It seemed ample enough.

The street was made up of a hodgepodge of two- or three-story homes. Unlike the trim, orderly brownstones of other Brooklyn neighborhoods, this was an assortment of modest frame designs, some of brick, some of wood, some of slate, some with flat roofs, some with slanted roofs, a blend of all colors. Some had small front yards and little gates, some went right to the sidewalk. The zoning commissioner was absent the day they did Howard Avenue.

It was a lower-middle-class block, and the word *elegant* was never used there. Fathers worked for other people, in blue-collar jobs. There were no professionals, and little need for suits and ties unless there was a funeral or a bar mitzvah or a wedding. Mothers took care of the kids. We thought they "didn't work."

Eddie and Jennie had a son they named Irwin, who was, by all accounts, an exceptional child. He was a second grader by age five. There was much talk in the apartment of how to deal with such a prodigy, how to find an appropriate school for such a wiz. But in 1932, when Irwin was six, he died of a ruptured appendix.

One can imagine the grief in the home, even at a time when child mortality was more frequent. There was, apparently, some recrimination lingering over this tragedy. With appendix cases, one can be saved by acting with speed. Either one or both of my parents must have felt some deep neglect of parental duty in failing to get Irwin proper medical attention. The appendix probably should not have ruptured. Irwin was buried in a cemetery near Belmont Racetrack, and his name seldom came up in future years. There must have been an understanding, spoken or silent, that there was blame somewhere for this great loss, and the less said the better. Thus, little in our home reminded my parents of Irwin, the big brother I never knew.

I was born a year later, on November 19, 1933. Lawrence Harvey Zeiger. Beth El Hospital. My father had prayed for a son, and his prayers had been answered. I wasn't given a middle name Irwin, although it is common among Jewish families to name someone after a deceased relative. It will probably not surprise you to know that I was overly protected, and at the slightest itch was off to the doctor.

At three, I developed a mastoid infection in my ear. You don't hear this expression much today, but it was enough to defer you from military service at one time. This was because it required the puncturing of the eardrum to drain the pus out, and in case of war, gas could somehow penetrate the punctured area and disable you. So the mastoidectomy was a reasonably big deal for a three-year-old, and I was rushed to the doctor's office.

I still remember the doctor using the word "surgery," and the mad cab ride from his office to the hospital. The doctor followed behind in his own car. I kept peeking out of the back window to make sure he was there. The earache hurt, and the fear of "surgery" and "hospital" were great. My parents were quiet, save for reassurances to me. My father even said they were taking me to the circus. One can easily imagine what they were thinking. It had been four years since they had taken Irwin to the hospital. A mastoid infection wasn't life-threatening, but they obviously had reached that same conclusion about Irwin's stomachache.

I survived the surgery and did not lose my hearing. But my mother remained overly consumed with my health. If I had a cold, there was aspirin and no school. Keep warm, stay in bed, drink plenty of fluids and chicken soup. If anything, no matter how slight, was wrong, I was pampered, spoiled, and worried over.

This sort of activity contributed to my hypochondriac tendencies in later years. I never miss a pill. A cold is a major tragedy because it was a major tragedy to my mother. Don't catch cold. Don't catch cold. Button your top button. Wear your scarf. Wear your gloves. Don't go out — you just took a shower. The one-hour rule: you can't go outside for an hour after showering, because your pores are open and you can catch cold. There was much talk of pores. And whatever happens, don't eat milk with meat because it will make your stomach curdle.

My father was an even-tempered man, but he knew his responsibilities as a parent and exercised them when he had to. He hit me twice.

I had fallen off the iron fence in front of our apartment,

and I was home from school nursing and admiring my broken arm. Iron fences were big in Brooklyn, our answer to the little wooden picket fences of country dreams. Lena Horne, who came from the Bedford section of Brooklyn, always spoke lovingly of those shiny black fences, each spike topped by an arrow-shaped point. I should have known better than to be climbing one.

I was sitting on the stoop, minding my own business, when a car pulled up in front. It was a big black car (they were all black then), and the driver looked suspicious. I was about eight, and I had been warned about talking to strangers, let alone approaching their cars.

The window was open on the passenger side, and he yelled to me, "Hey kid, come over here; I've got something for you."

Now this was the ultimate "DO NOT DO THIS," according to the rules of Brooklyn.

"What happens, Label," my parents would say, employing my Yiddish name, "if someone says he has candy for you?"

And I would duly answer, "I'd run away." My assumption was that there were hundreds of these strangers prowling the streets of Brooklyn looking for boys like me. They would snatch them away, never to be seen again. Next to not playing with matches, running from strangers was right up there.

So I looked at the man and said, "What do you have?" I figured I could find out and still make a run for it. And I knew if he said, "Candy," I was outta there.

He got out of the car. He was a huge guy in a dark raincoat. He walked around to the back door and popped it open. What he had was every comic book ever known to mankind. Comic books that hadn't even been printed yet. Hundreds of comics. The ultimate collection. Some so old and rare they might have been printed by Ben Franklin.

Well, I've got a problem now. The advice about strangers, I told myself, dealt specifically with candy. I don't remember anything about comics. And this was, after all, educational. It was reading material, at least. It wouldn't rot my teeth.

It seemed his son had misbehaved, and as a punishment, he was to lose his collection of comics to the first boy that his father encountered. Was this too severe a punishment for whatever the boy had done? Who cared. It was my good fortune to be home from school with my broken arm, while all the other potential suitors for this treasure were off in class at P.S. 28. Tough luck. So the deck was stacked. I thought this was an act of reward for my suffering with the broken arm. God was evening the score for that week, and he was up to Zeiger.

I thanked the gentleman, who now looked less ferocious, and broken arm and all, carted my goodies up to my room, little by little.

When my father came home from "the store," as he called it, I couldn't wait to tell him of my good fortune. Up the stairs I led him. I told him the whole story.

Wham. I got the back of his hand across my face. I flew across the room. And of course, I had to endure the lecture which began, "How many times have we told you . . ."

But he let me keep the comic books, so on balance, it was worth it.

The other time I got hit was a time I played hooky from Hebrew school. It was my bad luck to have been spotted by a friend of my father's, who promptly dropped into the saloon to deliver the news.

When my father got home that night, he asked me how Hebrew school was that day.

It was not an unusual question, so I gave it my usual answer.

"Fine."

Wham. Another smack across the face, another trip across the room.

"Don't you ever, ever lie to me," he said.

I didn't.

My brother Marty was born four years after me. I wasn't crazy about this development, especially when it appeared that some attention was going to be paid to him at my expense. I'd had a pretty good ride to that point — how did this kid figure to add to the fun? I was very jealous of him.

He was very cute, with blond, curly hair, and at seven months, it was decided to hire a professional to take photographs of him. I was in the room with Martin in his carriage as my parents entered with the photographer. And the three of them walked right by me without even acknowledging my presence.

I was always good for a pinch on the cheek or a rub of the hair from my father, but now even he was only focused on the little brat in the carriage.

Now, opportunity beckoned. The three adults left the room, and my mother told me to "watch Martin."

Watch him? I'd been watching him for seven months, and nothing good had come of it. I was pushing five years old and not getting the attention I deserved. The nervy photographer was the last straw.

So I picked Marty out of his carriage and decided to throw him out the window and onto the street.

It was, for a moment, a very powerful feeling and a very real drive. But fortunately, common sense prevailed, and I put him back. I don't think to this day Marty knows the whole story behind those baby pictures of his.

*   *   *

My father was a Yankee fan. I never knew why, except that the Yankees, by their name and by their great success, were the "all-American team," and, like many immigrants, Eddie had become a very patriotic man. He always flew the flag on patriotic occasions, loved George M. Cohan tunes, and thought owning his own "store" was the American dream come true. The Yankees, to him, must have symbolized that patriotism.

To be a Yankee fan in Brooklyn, where Ebbets Field was our Church of England, and the Dodgers belonged not to McKeever or MacPhail or Rickey or O'Malley, but to all of us, was to be on the outside looking in. We talked about it. We talked about a lot of things with very special walks we would take together down Howard Avenue to Saratoga Park.

Saratoga Park had a scent all its own, a little park in the middle of this working-class neighborhood called East New York. There were fully grown trees and grass and wildflowers. You had birds and squirrels and pigeons, and concrete-and-wood benches, and paths to walk which were not laid like sidewalk concrete, but with more care, with interlocking gray octagonal panels. It was harder not to step on the cracks, but you could be mesmerized by the patterns as you let your eyes focus from first one panel and then the adjoining ones, until you suddenly were studying the convergence of nine.

There was ice cream in the park, and Eddie was always a sport when it came to ice cream, as long as I didn't tell Mom, because it was so close to dinner.

I never went to Saratoga Park with my mother, nor did I tag along if she wheeled Marty there. Saratoga Park was only for my father and myself.

Our conversations were about school, but the scope of them could also be larger than the confines of the neighborhood. "What a country, what a country," he'd say on more than one occasion. He loved the United States so much. He'd talk about baseball and the Yankees, with the magnificent Joe DiMaggio, the mighty Lou Gehrig, and the wondrous Lefty Gomez. He went to Gehrig's funeral in June of 1941. He told me what a great man Franklin Roosevelt was, and how glad he was to be out of Europe at a time like this. He asked me what I'd learned in Hebrew school. When I hear my father's voice today, deep in my memories and in the recesses of my mind, it is his voice as it was in Saratoga Park.

We weren't wealthy, but not once did I ever think of us as poor, nor did I ever hear my father suggest as much. In fact, he thought we had more wealth than he could ever have imagined, what with owning his own business. And he had a dream, a dream of someday moving the family to Bensonhurst, "to be near the water." Although Bensonhurst was not "on the water," it was closer to the water than the inner-city pocket of East New York. Ah, Bensonhurst. He made it sound like the French Riviera. "Someday, Label, maybe we'll move to Bensonhurst."

But East New York was okay with me. It was a safe area; I knew violence only once there, when a kid hit me with a pane of glass and a little piece lodged in my nose. It's still there.

I would stop by the saloon after school. The cops knew me because they were Eddie's friends. Someone would lift me up and put me on the bar. There would be the smell of the saloon and the friendliness of the customers. The race results from Aqueduct would be on. Did my father wager now and then? Why else would the race results be on the radio?

I loved delivery days, when the kegs would be hoisted off

trucks and rolled into place. There was such an excitement
to the activity.

"Babe Ruth's father had a bar in Baltimore," someone
told me. They failed to add that the Babe's parents, deeming
him unmanageable, had placed him in an orphanage. Such
knowledge probably would have frightened me.

There was a certain darkness to our neighborhood, brought
about by the presence of the elevated subway line over
Fulton Street — the el. For shopping, you were drawn to
Fulton, and I'd hold my mother's hand as she went about
her rounds, listening for the roar of the trains overhead,
seeing an occasional spark from the tracks fly out and land
on the street. I used to think, "What if the train fell off the
tracks and landed down here?"

Fulton Street was all hustle and bustle six days a week,
with people popping in and out of the modest, affordable
stores. You'd be in the bakery, the cleaner, the hardware
store, the appliance store, the liquor store, the grocery, the
butcher, combining your packages, paying with cash, covet-
ing pennies as much as quarters, arguing when something
that had been nine cents was now ten. You'd see your neighbors covering their rounds in opposite, random directions.
The smell of the bakery dominated the scent of the block.
Always, you were drawn there on your mission, perhaps for
a rye bread, perhaps today, for just a cookie.

People with European backgrounds often carried their
own reusable string bags, fattening them as their newly
acquired goods were added. Always you would look down
to avoid dog droppings. The dogs all seemed to be strays;
the cats all belonged to the stores.

*   *   *

December 7, 1941, was the day Pearl Harbor was hit by the Japanese. My best recollection, at age eight, was not understanding where Pearl Harbor was, and that it was in fact part of the United States. Hawaii wasn't a state. But it was explained to me, and the gravity of the situation became clear. Could California be next? We all gathered around the radio the next day to listen to President Roosevelt tell Congress that we were now in a state of war.

My father had no doubt about his plans. He wanted to enlist and get right into action. Such was his patriotism that matters like his store and his family quickly became secondary to the threat to national security.

But he was forty-one, the father of two boys, the sole support of his family. He was rejected.

Not to be deterred, he decided to go into defense work. And so he sold his store for next to nothing and took a job at a defense plant in Kearny, New Jersey. It was a night-shift job, and he'd get home about eight in the morning, help get me off to school, sleep, and still be home when I got home. He didn't leave for work until around ten at night. I liked this, although I missed having the bar to stop in, where I could feel like a big shot with all the policemen.

Kearny was a long way off. We didn't know of New Jersey, other than he had to take a bus and a train to get there and back. The Brooklyn Navy Yard was much closer, but for whatever reason, he was working in Kearny.

We moved from Howard Avenue to Hopkinson Avenue after a couple of years. It was a four-story walk-up in the same neighborhood. We lived on the third floor. I still went to P.S. 28, still played basketball on the blacktop adjoining the school, and still had my mother peering through the wire-mesh fence, waiting for the game to end so that she could walk me home. Life was better than ever; my father was home more than ever.

D-Day, the day we landed on Normandy, a success which would eventually lead to the end of the war in Europe, was on June 6, 1944. There was euphoria in the house, and a feeling that Eddie's work at the defense plant had, in some measure, been a part of this great landing.

Three days later, a Friday night, Eddie left for work. He had complained of chest pains earlier in the day, and went so far as to visit a doctor, but it was decided that he was merely suffering from indigestion, a not uncommon feeling in a Jewish household. On Saturday morning, I went to the library and took out my usual complement of ten books. I was a voracious reader, a wonderful student, and a pride to my parents. I was breezing through P.S. 28 and no doubt evoking memories of what Irwin might have been. Irwin was in second grade at age five; I had skipped second grade and gone from first to third.

As I got within eye's view of the apartment, I saw three police squad cars parked in front, flivvers, as they were called. I rushed to the door and heard my mother on the top floor, shrieking, "Oy, oy, no, no."

I knew the cops. They were crying. Cops crying. You don't see that much. They had been regulars at Eddie's, friends of my father's. One of them put his big arm around me and told me that we needed to go outside.

We got in his flivver together and he drove me to the Loews Pitkin. He took me to the movies. Robert Taylor was starring in *Bataan*.

It was at the movies that he told me that my father had had a heart attack on the bus and had died. He had died alone on the bus, without time to say good-bye, without time for one last look at his family.

I spent many hours with that wonderful policeman that day. We just drove around. I didn't say very much. He talked a lot about what a good friend my father had been. I didn't know what to do, say, or how to act. I was ten years old.

At about six, the policeman took me home. Marty was only six. He was confused by the events and wanted to know when Daddy would be coming home. Aunts, uncles, cousins, began arriving. They kept telling me that I was now the man of the house, a statement I deeply resented. They were trying to be nice, but such pronouncements did not help.

I didn't go to the funeral. It must have been determined that I was too young for such things. I spent that lonely afternoon bouncing a rubber Spaldeen ball off the front stoop. Someone must have been left with me, but I felt very alone. My father was barely forty-three. That must have seemed very old, very grown-up to me at the time. Now I know better.

They buried my father next to Irwin. My mother, the youngest of six girls, was the first to be widowed among them. A widow at forty-three.

Two weeks later, her mother, my grandmother, died. She had experienced a lot of death for a young woman. And I was halfway to being an orphan at age ten.

My silence at the unfolding events only masked an anger within me, or so I came to understand later. People saying, "Label, now you're a man, you have these responsibilities, you have to take care of your mother ..." only fueled the anger. How dare my father do this to me! These are understandable reactions, but, of course, very difficult for a ten-year-old to deal with. My life would forever change.

Every morning and every night I had to go to Hopkinson Synagogue to say Kaddish, the prayer for the dead. "*Yisgadal, v'yiskadash, sh'me, rabbo.*" Although the war had claimed many young men, most were not fathers. So there I was, praying with men in their forties and fifties, feeling very awkward, very out of place. You needed ten men to pray — a minyan — and if you were one short, you'd go out in the street and recruit someone.

A month after my father died, I was sent off to a camp in Kingston, New York. I didn't like being away. I was scared and lonely, and I missed my father terribly. And somehow, missing him in Brooklyn was better than missing him in Kingston.

So I asked some counselors and found out how to send a telegram, and I wired my mother to come and get me. And she did. A new relationship was forming, one in which my wishes were her commands. If she was protective of my health and safety to this point, she would now be at my beck and call for all my worldly wishes. I would learn this in a hurry. Her life was now her children.

We weren't going to stay on Hopkinson. My Aunt Bessie, my mother's sister, found a place across the street from her in, of all places, Bensonhurst. Bensonhurst, my father's dream community, was to be our new home. Except my father would not be there to share it.

THREE

BROOKLYN 14, NEW YORK

IT WAS IN BENSONHURST, mailing address Brooklyn 14, New York, that my senses and my memory both seemed to take hold together. It was the first place in which every experience was logged into my brain. It was where my friendships were formed, my dreams developed, my personality molded. If it wasn't the garden spot of the universe, it was as close as I'd come to it.

We went on relief. Today it's welfare. It should be called assistance, and it should permit you to supplement it with work. But inspectors came around to make sure you weren't cheating. Today, that means drawing a welfare check when you're able-bodied and just not looking for work. Back then, cheating meant earning something on the side to try and move to a better life.

Bensonhurst was a sunny, middle-class community, with a sense of suburbia in the heart of Brooklyn. Although there was an el running through the neighborhood, there was more hustle and bustle under the el on 86th Street than there had been under the more haunting el over Fulton

Street. People seemed happier, friendlier. I thought they made eye contact more; looked down for dog droppings less. Dogs were pets, not strays. A lot of fathers wore suits. Some mothers knew how to drive. There wasn't a sense of poor.

There were some six-story apartment buildings with buzzers and elevators, and there were smaller apartments with gardens and driveways. The streets had an openness and an order to them. You could even smell the ocean air. It was a garden-style apartment that Aunt Bessie found for us at 2136 83rd Street. We had the attic apartment, so while the building was perfect, dad's dream, we were really just the upstairs boarders. Bessie was across the street at 2133. She lived there with Uncle Charlie, a tailor, who liked to sit and rock on his porch. Bessie was a sweet, round, rotund woman, who was like a mother to my mother.

Eighty-third Street, of course, was nestled right in there between 82nd and 84th. Anyone could find his way around this neighborhood. There was a logic to the grid that formed our neighborhood; it was a perfect collection of rectangles, only interrupted on the east by the nuisance of Stillwell Avenue cutting diagonally north and south and forcing the ends of all of these numbered streets.

The smell of the ocean breeze was not imagined, particularly when it had the benefit of a southerly breeze. We were only about ten blocks from Gravesend Bay, an area you might know today as being just south of the massive Verrazano Narrows Bridge, where the New York Marathon starts each fall. There was no bridge when I lived there. Gravesend Bay was, of course, the beginning of the Atlantic Ocean. Next block east was in France.

If you took Stillwell Avenue to the end, you'd hit Coney Island, which was as good as urban recreation got in America. Disneyland was still a long way off. Coney Island was a wonderful escape for us, a magical paradise with food and games and the ocean and a boardwalk which went on forever, so if you needed to take a very long walk without any traffic lights, with just the smell of the ocean air and the sight of the sky and the waves of the Atlantic, this was the place. I was there on days when more than a million people went to cool off. To walk the beach on a day like that was to serpentine through blankets and umbrellas, looking for just one small spot to plant your next footstep, imagining beyond hope that you might find your own blanket again. The men wore baggy bathing trunks; the women, one-piece bathing suits with little skirts at the end. In incredible heat, fully dressed vendors in white with heavy metal storage boxes would peddle orange drinks and ice cream, and it had to be the worst job in the world.

Comic Jack Carter was born in Coney Island. He has told me of his surprise as a child of realizing that his very own neighborhood, a place taken for granted by those who lived there, was in fact a tourist area which people traveled great distances to reach. Summers were incredibly festive, and there were even stars at the Brighton Beach Theater to give the area a show-business feeling, stars like Jolson and Cantor.

Carter, in fact, began performing when he was just a child, unabashedly hoisted onto tabletops at his father's little candy store to perform for patrons.

You'd walk the Boardwalk in bare feet and stop to pull out splinters. You'd sample the cuisines of Feltman's and Nathan's, generally settling for their famed hot dogs. There were no hot dogs in the world like Nathan's, so plump and juicy, with mustard and sauerkraut, and soft rolls forming a perfect envelope for the little weiner. It was a four-bite lunch that filled you up. You could not walk past Nathan's without ordering one. The smell of a Nathan's hot dog was the equivalent of a national anthem for Brooklyn. We didn't have a borough song; we had a borough scent and taste.

You'd watch the roller coasters in the amusement parks and listen to the screams, look at the peaceful rides older folks would take on the Boardwalk's rolling chairs: Steeple-chase, the Parachute Jump, and Luna Park. All just minutes away from Bensonhurst.

Forming a square around our neighborhood were 18th Avenue to the west, Bay Ridge Parkway to the north, Bay Parkway to the east, and 86th Street to the south. They were the major streets, with 86th Street sitting below the el, housing all of our local stores, and, where it met Bay Parkway, forming not just a neat corner with the Bay Parkway el station, but "The Corner," where we would all gather and discuss the affairs of the day, growing up in front of one another in body and in mind.

Unlike Fulton Street, there were some bigger stores here, supermarkets, even. They were more populous and the customers came from a wider territory. The baker, the butcher, the hardware store, had big competitors, and you had to select which one was "yours." When the fumes from buses weren't overpowering the bakery smells, you were again drawn to Ebinger's, to sample a little blackout cake, crumb bun, or lemon cupcake. A box from Ebinger's, pale green with brown striping, was the mark of a successful shopping trip.

Our street, one block in from Bay Parkway, was a two-lane road with room for on-street parking. But with public transportation so near, so convenient, and so safe, no one in the neighborhood felt the car to be a necessity, and our streets were never overcrowded with automobiles. There were times we could play ball on the street without any concern for parked cars, and little concern for the occasional interruption of a passing motorist.

The larger area, the full geography of Bensonhurst, was bounded by 14th Avenue at the northwest, 61st Street and MacDonald Avenue to the northeast, Avenue U and 26th Street to the southeast, and Gravesend Bay in the southwest. The area got its name from a Benson family, potato farmers who lived in the area prior to the Civil War.

All the homes on our block were modest in size, with little front yards, small back yards, and even some driveways tucked in between buildings, leading to detached garages. There were trees and flowers and people cared about what neighbors thought about the appearance of their properties.

The streets themselves, 86th Street down to the sixties, stretch all the way into Bay Ridge, a nice community to the west separated by the ugly-sounding Gowanus Expressway.

Peter Max, the great pop artist, came to Bensonhurst by way of Berlin, Shanghai, Tibet, Italy, Haifa, and Paris. Of all of these exotic places, he told me, Bensonhurst was his favorite.

"It was so hip," he said. "I think it was the Jews and the Italians, the mixture, that made it so creative. Even the crime was creative."

Peter's first memory was coming to live with his Aunt Zeisel on Bay 26th Street. The first word he learned was *boychik*. Aunt Zeisel was a strong woman who lived to a hundred and eight. One day shortly after Peter arrived, she sent him to the store and said, "Get me a mirror."

Peter returned with a little pocket mirror.

"No, no," said Aunt Zeisel, "a *Mirror,* with Winchell." She wanted the New York *Mirror.*

After graduating from Lafayette a couple of years after me, Peter's professional art career took off when he was hired to illustrate the covers of pulp Western novels. As his models, he used Bay Parkway guys and put them in cowboy clothing. They were even called the Bay Parkway Cover Boys, and some went on to Hollywood as models, actors, or extras.

If my mother was not a strong woman up to this point, she would now become one. She had come to America as the youngest of six girls, and she was now the only one classified as a widow. So although there would be strength required for her to manage a home and raise two boys, she did have five sisters looking over her shoulder at every turn.

Her parents had settled in the Lower East Side of New York when they arrived, in 1909. Her father was tall, with blue eyes, red hair, and a red beard. If I let my beard grow out, it's reddish. That's where it comes from. I probably inherited his height, too. I didn't know him well; he died when I was very young, but we always had family circle meetings, and he was always talked about as though he was still there.

At family circle meetings, the men would run things, but the women were active participants, while the kids ran amuck. The adults sat in a circle, hence the name, and took this all very seriously as though the family was a corporation with certain obligations to its membership. My Uncle Jack, who had a tuxedo-rental business, usually presided, and they would take the form of board of directors meetings, with agendas, new business, old business, who was ill and should be visited, who was celebrating a special occasion, when was the unveiling of Aunt so-and-so's gravestone, plus a little infusion of gossip. I didn't like these meetings very much; they were not "kid-friendly," and we were constantly told to keep away from the food until it was time to eat, but I remember secretly longing to jump on the body of my cousin Rosie and having a thing for my cousin Loretta's legs.

My mother was a pretty, dark-haired woman and a skilled seamstress. She was slim and short, wore lipstick, had a sense of style if not the money to support it, and had a wonderful sense of humor and a nice singing voice.

Today I realize that, at forty-three, my mother was still a young and attractive woman with needs and desires, and she might well have remarried. But Marty and I were determined that that would never happen. When she finally got around to having gentlemen callers, the two of us would act so embarrassingly that we'd drive away any thoughts they might entertain about making this a more meaningful relationship.

We'd run around, throw things on the floor, fight with each other, and yell at Mom. Anyone dating her would realize that we were part of the deal, and therefore not return. It was terribly cruel, but deep down, my mother understood, and never seemed to mind.

Her children were her life. This was an overwhelming sense that we shared with Italian families. Jewish and Italian mothers, the two we were most exposed to, had gone through the incredible experience of uprooting their families from Europe and making that enormous journey to the unknown, to America. Huddled in their boats, they had probably sensed the feeling of family, and of parents protecting children, more than one ordinarily might. And I believe that from this came this great bonding instinct, which always made the child more important than the parent. There are portions of it I feel today, when I tell my twenty-four-year-old daughter to bundle up in the cold weather.

These values were not unique to Jews and Italians, but they were the people I was most associated with. Black families in Brooklyn had strong family values, as Lou Gossett, Jr., has explained.

Lou, who was once a short-order cook on the Coney Island Boardwalk, calls it a "protective umbrella," under which neighbors might at times assume family roles in looking after kids. If a kid stepped out of line, the mother would be alerted and the neighbors would huddle to determine appropriate action.

My mother was the youngest of six girls, and she must have felt this protection not only from her parents, but from five siblings as well. And when she grew into womanhood, and she cared for her mother, and then for her children, that sense of "them first" was always pervasive.

I think relief paid us $38 a month, plus the rent, which went directly to the Licaris, who lived downstairs and owned the place. My father had left no insurance.

Sal and Mary Licari were wonderful landlords and helped to look after my mother, knowing her situation. They grew tomatoes over the driveway, and always had some for us. Mary Licari and my mother often went shopping together, arm in arm, down to 86th Street, except they would go their separate ways when it came time for the butcher. Mom went kosher.

Mom would always buy Grade A meat from the kosher butcher, despite our little fixed income. She would forsake things for herself so we could have Grade A. The inspectors would show up and say, "Mrs. Zeiger, why are you buying top-grade meat?" They'd actually look in the icebox and ask questions like that.

Mom got a Singer sewing machine and took in some

sewing on the side. People would bring dresses to be hemmed. It couldn't have provided much, but every penny counted. And if the relief inspectors were coming, I remember the Licaris helping to cover for us. Mrs. Licari would say, "Relief inspector!" and we would hide the machine and the sewing. If they came in and saw the machine, they'd say, "This isn't a size-ten dress; this isn't yours!" So we'd stall for time, say things like the door is stuck, all the time hiding the evidence while the relief inspector cooled his heels downstairs.

The late Jack Gilford had a mother who worked in the garment trade, too. Jack described his mother's religion as being neither Jewish nor Christian, but "Not Starving," and thus she was always looking to augment her modest income as a cloak-and-suit finisher. One day, a presser at the suit shop taught her how to prepare a special, low-cost "no-meat casserole," made up of fermented potatoes, prunes, sugar, and water, which would, in turn, be distilled into whiskey. So his mother became a bootlegger, selling the product under the table. My mother would never do such a thing, and was able to get by on relief and the warnings from the Licaris.

The City of New York bought me my first pair of glasses. When the time came that I needed them, relief gave you a slip of paper and you went to Busch Opticians on 14th Street in Manhattan. They were the biggest opticians in New York, the only ones with a chain of stores. But you couldn't go to the one in Brooklyn, you had to go into Manhattan with your slip of paper to the branch in Manhattan that took care of the relief customers. There, my eyes were examined, and I received my first pair of wire-rimmed glasses, free, that told all the world that you were poor and on relief and couldn't afford a pair with frames.

I hated the fact that I had to wear these glasses. It was like a badge. As I said, we never thought of ourselves as poor, and until this point, I never had any reason to think about it or acknowledge it to others.

Wire rims were not a fashion statement. I always removed them for photos. And when they'd break, it was another slip of paper, and back to 14th Street for a new pair.

The trip to the city, while less than a half hour by express train, was a trip to another world. The buildings were huge, the people impersonal, all seemingly in a rush to get somewhere. But the excitement of it all was thrilling; even a mission for eyeglasses took on the appeal of a Saturday adventure matinee at the movies. You would emerge from the train as though moved by a time machine into another decade, where life was lived at a different pace, everything was bigger and wider, traffic was thicker, drivers more impatient, and a sense of danger, much more imagined than real, kept you on the lookout for odd-looking people, who were always in abundance.

Relief lasted only about a year and a half, and then my mother took a job in a sweatshop in Brooklyn as a seamstress. She joined the International Ladies Garment Workers Union. It was a dress-manufacturing plant, and I visited her there on occasion, saw her at the end of the row, all the sewing machines humming away. She got to be the foreman of her line. Aunt Bessie would look after Marty and me when we got home from school.

Not to be confused with Aunt Bessie was Auntie Bella, whose title was lovingly bestowed, not a birthright. She was the love of my life, a Scottish/English Protestant woman who had worked for my father back in East New York, and who now helped care for us. She would often stay for a week, then go home, stay another time, help out, go home. I loved this woman, the woman who taught us about Christmas. If she was with us at Christmastime, my mother encouraged her to celebrate her holiday. We were the only family in the neighborhood with a Christmas tree, we exchanged Christmas gifts, and this was all because of Auntie Bella. We had a kosher home and a Christmas tree! To this day, I still love the holiday, love the Christmas music. It's the saddest and the happiest time for me, just as it is for so many people around the world.

Once Auntie Bella had a niece who dressed as Santa and visited our home. Marty and I were small, and we both believed that this was truly Santa. We told all the kids the next day, and defended his honor.

Bella had a genuine letter from President Lincoln. Her father had headed the Illinois Brigade during the Civil War and attained the rank of captain. Lincoln had a sweet habit of writing to any officer who was wounded during the war, as best as he could keep up. The letter said something like: "Dear Captain Bairron: Your meritorious service to our nation is most appreciated, and I wish you well, etc. Sincerely, A. Lincoln." Let me tell you, collectors offered her plenty for that letter, but money was not important to her. I suspect she was buried with the letter.

She was a proud, proud American. Memorial Day used to be called Decoration Day, and Auntie Bella always wore an appropriate carnation to honor her father and marched in the parade in Prospect Park, our beautiful acreage in the middle of Brooklyn that was designed by the same man who designed Central Park, Frederick Law Olmsted.

When she was about ninety-five, she was sitting with me watching with marvel as I watched the Dodger game on our new Emerson television, which we had treated ourselves to in honor of Marty's bar mitzvah. "You mean this is happening right now?" She couldn't believe it. At one point I started yelling at the TV set that the umpire had blown it, the ball was fair, not foul, and she merely said, "Why don't you write them a letter?"

Auntie Bella never married, and lived nearly a hundred years. I'm sure she died a virgin. She used to say, "No man will ever touch me." I was at home when she passed away, around 1950, and I remember answering the phone and hearing her doctor tell me the news. She died in her sleep. I cried then, because she had been such an integral part of my childhood.

My personality changed after my father died. I think I can trace it to my bar mitzvah. After Dad died, I continued going to Hebrew school faithfully every day, partly recalling the time he'd hit me for lying, but mostly because I always did the right thing. My father had kept me disciplined, and always I wanted to make my parents proud of me. The one exception may have been my rebelling against going to school, but here, my father cleverly intervened by going to the principal and requesting that I be made eraser monitor. This humble task, often considered a punishment by others, somehow made school pleasant for me. My father had been the hero; he had devised a minor role for me which made it okay to go to school. When he died, that little faith that he would find the solution to keep me honest seemed to go with him.

My mother kept the faith; we had two sets of dishes at home, *milchedig* and *flayshedig,* for meat and dairy meals. My first recollection of my new neighborhood was the new synagogue where I attended Hebrew school and the Hopkinson synagogue where I said Kaddish each evening. People felt sorry for me there. I was barely twelve; everyone else was in his forties or fifties. After school I'd be playing with the guys, then excuse myself and go off to pray. Bensonhurst was maybe 40 percent Jewish, 40 percent Italian, 20 percent Irish. There were no Protestants, except for when Auntie Bella visited. I barely knew about Protestantism. To me, Christians were Catholics. It was the same word.

Instead of carrying a deep sorrow for being the only kid in the neighborhood without a father, I began to use it to my advantage. I knew I could evoke sympathy when I wanted to. I felt it at Kaddish. I knew I could get away with just a little more than the next guy.

At my bar mitzvah, which took place at a synagogue in Borough Park at 55th Street and 14th Avenue, I read my long haftorah splendidly, and then gave a little speech, invoking the memory of Eddie Zeiger, and how proud this day would have made him. I could tell I was moving the congregation. I appeared near tears to the audience, but in my heart, I knew I wasn't really crying. I was still dealing with an anger I didn't understand. I really got into that speech. I could feel the crowd swaying to my every word and every emotion. I had them.

I believe from that time forth, I made a decision to make the best of my situation for all it was worth.

I also realized, standing at the pulpit that day, that I was going to be on the radio. From the age of five I had dreamed of it. That magical box which brought so much entertainment and information beckoned me. I would roll up comic books and pretend they were microphones. No one took me seriously at five. But at thirteen, standing there winning over an audience with my voice, I took myself seriously, and the people in the synagogue took me seriously. I never had a doubt from that day forward that I would be on the radio someday. I never entertained a day's thought about any other profession.

Joe Paterno, the great Penn State football coach, grew up in an Italian neighborhood in Brooklyn and gives a good example of how Italians and Jews understood each other and got along well together. Italians understood about the High Holy Days and bar mitzvahs, and, for the more religious Jews, were available as *Shabbes goys,* people who would turn the lights off and on on the Sabbath if your brand of Orthodoxy forbade it.

Composer Aaron Copland was bar mitzvahed on Tompkins Place at Baith Israel Anshei Emes, Brooklyn's "mother synagogue." It was a forty-five-minute walk for his family, and his reception was held in his father's department store, a fair-sized establishment on Washington Avenue. The reception, involving moving all the merchandise aside to make room for the guests, was Copland's greatest memory of the day. Mine was my speech.

My mother, meanwhile, was more concerned about eating than anything else. Even when I was married she was like this. One day, after I'd moved to Miami, she called my wife, Alene. Alene made the mistake of saying that I had a bad cold.

"Oh, really?" she said. "Put him on."

So I take the phone and she says, "Larry, it's your mother, listen, you don't have to talk, I'll understand, just tell me, is she feeding you well? Just say yes or no."

Her sisters were like this, too. Aunt Dora was the master chef in the family, and the world's foremost foremost. She'd throw doctors out of the house if she thought they didn't know what they were talking about. She was some tough lady. One day I've got a job delivering tuxedos, and I was going to be in her neighborhood. So since my mother always said, "If you're ever near one of my sisters, call," I called to say I'd like to stop in and say hello. And I knew to add, "Don't fix anything, I can only stay a couple of minutes." I told her I'd be over in about twenty minutes.

I was there in twenty minutes. Every pot was boiling. She had prepared a five-course meal. Chicken soup, salad with oil-and-vinegar dressing, gefilte fish, a pot roast with sweet potatoes and spinach, crumb cake, milk. Eat! Eat! She had to hoist me out the door.

Meal times were essentially me and Marty, with Mom serving us and barely sitting down for a minute. She was up and down, up and down, bringing more, only gulping down something for herself while we were consuming our portions. She would sit and watch us eat, making sure we chewed our food properly and left nothing over. If you left one crumb of pie over, she'd feel rejected, because she had baked it and wanted it to be devoured. To leave something on the plate was not only wasteful but insulting to the cook and bad for your health. Forever went the clanging of dishes, coming and going. I have no memory of all three of us seated through a full meal. Can't picture it. Nor do I have the slightest memory of ever once bringing the dishes to the sink, or washing them, or drying them, or putting them away, or setting the table. Same for cleaning my room, making my bed, putting my laundry in the hamper, volunteering for any unpleasant home chore. So dedicated was my mother that I even have memories of her following me around the apartment with an ashtray when I started to smoke. I would not have been a poster boy for helping out at home. Not only were we never asked to help out, our mother derived so much pleasure from the care of her children that she encouraged this behavior through her actions. Not once did I hear her complain that "they never lift a finger," and she never said such a thing to my friend Herbie, with whom she had many long, meaningful, and private discussions. No, if she could simply bring a smile to Larry's or Marty's face, this was pleasure enough for her. Her children were her life.

I grew up with all food well done. Veal cutlets, well done, dripping with fat. Breaded, greasy, and thin. If you eat this and don't have a heart attack, you'll live a long life. Lamb chops, well done, with plenty of fat. Steak, well done. To this day, I don't know from red meat. The best I can manage today is medium well.

I have wonderful memories of my mother's specialties. Noodle kugel, a pudding of noodles and eggs, sometimes with fruit and sugar and cinnamon. You'd cook up the noodles, drain the water, mix in the ingredients, and bake. Matzobrei. Soak two squares of matzo in water, drain, add three eggs, salt, and fry it into a pancake or a scrambled eggs consistency. I would kill for matzobrei. Kasha varnishkas I could eat forever. With bow ties. The kasha would come either fine, medium, or coarse, and I liked coarse. It was a kind of brown barley cereal. Liver, which most people hated, I loved. The butcher would give you free liver if you spent $10 with him. Since my heart attack a few years ago, liver is one thing I've been told to stop. I miss it a lot.

Outside the house, take me right under the el stop at Brighton Beach for Shatskin's potato knishes — and wonderful blintzes — blueberry ones and cheese ones. You can eat six or seven, then get right in your car and drive to the hospital for your heart attack. Oh, the heartburn of Jewish cooking. We had Tums for dessert regularly.

*   *   *

You entered our apartment up a flight of stairs and into a small foyer. To the left was a living room, with everything covered in plastic slipcovers. Through it, to the right, Mom's bedroom, overlooking 83rd Street. To the right of the foyer, the rear of the house was the kitchen, to which a back staircase led, and then our bedroom, with a fire escape outside the window, overlooking a driveway. The fire escape was a refuge on many hot nights, and the sound of Red Barber doing the Dodgers games is vivid in my memories of those nights.

The place was always spotless, and my mother was famous for her highly waxed linoleum.

This being the top-floor apartment, the ceiling in our bedroom was slanted. That led itself to interesting wall coverings for Marty and myself. He used to collect St. Louis Cardinal photos and arrange them so that they would form a perfect pattern, emulating the slant. On my side were the Brooklyn Dodger head shots, black and white, with my favorite, Billy Cox, front and center, the most favorable position from my pillow.

As you would expect, my mother's family became my extended family. My mother was a great hostess, and our apartment was always a beehive of visiting relatives, partially looking out for her, partially enjoying the pleasure of her company. My mother's five sisters were Yetta, Dora, Bessie, Rose, and Anna.

Aunt Yetta was the oldest sister. She never learned English. Her husband, Izzy, was the oldest man I ever knew, even though he was only in his fifties. He was a junk dealer, and when he'd visit, he'd usually have some trinkets for us from his line of work: broken alarm clocks, toy soldiers with

broken rifles, games with missing spinners, harmonicas with
a little rust, toy fire-marshall badges without clips, comic
books without covers.

Izzy would come in and head straight for the sofa. He'd
slowly drop into it with moans of *"Oy vey, oy vey."* He'd sigh
and belch and generally plop there until it was time to leave.
I'm the same age today that Izzy was then. I can't believe
anyone could be so old so young.

I had a cousin named Al Gorenstein. He had been a
prisoner of war during World War II. He had been captured
by Rommel, and he called it the best thirty days of his life.

"When you were a prisoner of Rommel's," he told us,
"they'd ask you your name, rank, and serial number. When
they found out I was an officer, the questions would end.
Rommel followed the Geneva convention; an officer was to
be treated as an officer. I was taken to join the German
officers in their mess tent. And the German enlisted men
had to salute you. So I'd go from a tent to have lunch with
Rommel, and he'd have about twelve of his guys there, and
the food was fantastic. Best I ever ate. And we'd sit around
and wonder how long we could get away with this until we
were rescued. I wasn't so sure I wanted to be rescued."

My Aunt Rose lived three blocks away, on 80th Street,
with my Uncle Jack, a furrier, and a collie named Tippy. I
sometimes delivered furs for Uncle Jack after school, and
after Aunt Rose had a stroke and became my first aunt to die,
Jack moved to Florida. I lived with him when I first went to
Miami, in 1957.

President Roosevelt died on April 12, 1945. He was the only
President I'd ever known. His framed picture hung on a wall
in our apartment. You don't see a lot of that anymore.

My mother worshipped him. To her, he was Jewish, or at

least he represented himself as being Jewish at heart to Jewish people. She wouldn't believe a lot of things about him, that maybe he'd turned away the Ship of Hope carrying Jewish immigrants, or maybe that he knew about the Nazi death camps.

The day he died, I was on the way to Hebrew school, and I saw people crying in the streets. Director Paul Mazursky, who lived in Brownsville, vividly recalls people sitting on their stoops and weeping. When he directed *Next Stop, Greenwich Village,* he developed a character based on those stoop-sitters.

My mother was at work, and I went to her shop to tell her the news. But of course, they already knew, and all the women were sitting there, sewing and crying. It was like losing a family member. He was like everyone's favorite uncle, who would somehow provide when times got tough. To the Catholics, he was like a patron saint. The whole neighborhood felt his loss.

Arthur Godfrey's voice was the one I remember describing FDR's death on the radio. He described the funeral with the "hearse now turning onto Pennsylvania Avenue. And there is the horse with no rider. And everyone is so sad."

I remember Edward R. Murrow brilliantly describing the events on CBS radio. I remember him telling of the rain, and how right that seemed for such a sad day. I fantasized that I was the announcer describing the events. Roosevelt dead? We didn't even know he was sick. We didn't even know he was crippled. In this pre-TV age, he always appeared healthy and vigorous, and the press protected his paralysis from the public. Never was he photographed in his wheelchair. We knew he had polio, knew of his trips to Warm Springs, Georgia, for treatments, knew he sat a lot behind his desk, and sat in the front row for group pictures at summit meetings, sat in his car, but sick? No way.

Then Truman's voice came on the air. What a letdown. Roosevelt was so eloquent on radio. Truman had no spark, nothing. This would take a lot of getting used to.

But by 1948, our feelings had changed. We got to like Truman a lot. He was the underdog, the type of guy you loved to root for in Brooklyn. He was like the Dodgers, exceeding expectations. He had to fill Roosevelt's shoes, and by God, he did it. Here was this little haberdasher with glasses from Missouri, wherever that was, suddenly the leader of the free world. And he pulled it off! We hated Dewey, and one of the happiest days of my life was the day Truman upset Dewey and retained the presidency. I remember the frenzy of the campaign, with people actually yelling, "Give 'em hell, Harry," at speeches. On the day he won, I remember that we all stood and cheered and applauded at our school desks, as the results were not known until the morning, when we were in class. Never mind that Dewey was from New York; he was a hated Republican fruitcake (even though he was from their moderate wing), and we just couldn't warm up to this aristocratic-looking guy who didn't speak our language. Truman was a feisty, Brooklyn kind of guy, who told you where you stood. He took no crap from anyone, not even from General MacArthur, and when he said, "The buck stops here," you said, "Yes, sir."

The Bensonhurst people, the Jews, Italians, and Irish, had especially revered Roosevelt. They hated Herbert Hoover and the Republican Party. The Republicans probably got 5 percent of the vote during the years I lived in Bensonhurst. There was no two-party system, and my mother never did understand how Jacob Javits, the Jewish Senator from New

York, could have been a Republican. She almost voted for him, but she couldn't bring herself to do it in the end.

My mother was wildly liberal, and very much influenced by the New York *Post*. I was influenced, in turn, by her, and the first time I ever voted, in 1956, it was on the Liberal line, row C.

Herbie Cohen was the first friend I made in the new neighborhood. If Brooklyn has produced its share of characters, Herbie may head the list. A better friend no man ever had.

There was a stage in my life that I wanted to be Herbie. He had a father whom I liked a lot. His father, Morris Cohen, owned a business making bindings for hats, and he worked like hell but made good money. I would guess maybe $20,000 a year, which was really something when you personally aspired to someday make $200 a week. The Cohens were among the first to have a TV and the first to have a car. They had a little summer home in New Jersey. But none of them ever acted uppity. Herbie's mother, Esther, still alive today and in her nineties, was a close friend to my mother. The Cohens lived in an apartment building a couple of blocks from me, at the corner of 85th Street and 21st Avenue.

Everybody lived in apartment buildings. Home ownership was something so far from the realm of imagination we never even considered it. Here's your neighborhood, here's your apartment, this is your rent. That was just the way life was supposed to be.

Al Kelly, the old double-talk artist, had this bit where he'd say, "Imagine if home ownership was always there, and then somebody invented the concept of rent. Think of it folks, no outlay, no mortgage, no big down payment. Just $150 a

month and all this can be yours!" Or he'd talk about cigarette lighters coming first, and then somebody invents the
match. "That's right, folks, no more wicks, no more messy
fluids, no more exploding flames. The match. It's safe. It's
disposable. It's simple to use. Just flick it, light it, and throw
it away. And folks — it's free with every purchase of cigarettes!"

Herbie was a provocateur. He was a schemer and a trou-
blemaker, but he was in it for the sport, and he got just as
much satisfaction from getting into trouble as getting out of
it. Crime for Herbie was nothing more than humming in
class and leaving the teacher to wonder who was causing
the disturbance.

Nothing would ever stop Herbie. When we had to join
the General Organization in school to attend assemblies
and participate in activities, Herbie decided, "Let's not join
the G.O. Let's see what they can do to us." The thrill of the
campaign was as important to Herbie as the result, win or
lose.

He never lost that spirit. It's with him today. In 1980, I had
a press credential to be on the floor at the Democratic
National Convention, at Madison Square Garden in New
York. That was the year Ted Kennedy was challenging Jimmy
Carter for the presidential nomination. Security was as tight
as it had ever been at a convention, especially with tensions
high and New York being a difficult town.

"I'll meet you on the convention floor," said Herbie,
when I called him to say I was in town.

"Herbie, you don't understand. I can't get you a pass.
Everything is triple-checked here. Ed Muskie got thrown out
yesterday because he didn't have a red badge. He's the Secretary of State. There's a security guard at every entrance. I'll
meet you outside the Garden for a bite."

Herbie doesn't know the meaning of "can't." "See you on the floor tomorrow," he said.

I managed to get him a yellow badge to get him into the building, but I couldn't get a red floor pass. No way. We were supposed to have a U.S. Senator on our radio show as a guest; he couldn't get through. He didn't have a red badge.

Herbie just walked into the Garden, found a likely looking entrance ramp to the floor, and marched full of confidence up to the stunned guard. He slapped him hard on the back and said, "Great job," and wham, he's on the convention floor. And the guard just stood there with a huge smile on his face. I looked up and it was Herbie.

The next time I saw that look was seven years later, February 24, 1987. I had had a heart attack in the morning and was operated on that day at George Washington University Medical Center. Herbie got paged at National Airport. And somehow, when he got paged, he had a sense that something was wrong with Larry. We're like brothers in that way. We know. He called his wife, Ellen, and she said, "Larry's in the hospital." He canceled his flight and came straight over.

He was greeted by my daughter, Chaia. "Dad's resting in intensive care," she said. "No one can go in." Chaia should have known better. Herbie hadn't canceled his flight to sit in a waiting room.

I was all hooked up to a hundred tubes and IVs, and I look up and it's Herbie. The greatest face I ever saw. He had beaten the no-visitors-in-intensive-care system at George Washington University Medical Center. This was no small achievement. This was one formidable figure.

One day, when we were kids, Herbie got it into his mind that he wanted to build a raft and go sailing off Gravesend

Bay. Although the smell of the ocean would occasionally permeate our midst, we never really thought of ourselves as nautical. But Herbie had been inspired by a guy down the block named Stewie Schwabel, who had a boat, and who set sail for Africa. The fact that he was reported missing, then fished out of the sea by the Coast Guard and returned four days later, did not daunt Herbie's perception of the assignment. On a map, the ocean just didn't look that insurmountable. Herbie did get his raft to the water, but not much farther. In the end, good sense won out.

I mentioned this to Henny Youngman one day, how we were not especially nautical in our thinking, as we might have been had we lived in, say, Maine. Henny lived closer to the water, at 223 51st Street. He had more vivid memories of sitting on the docks and watching the boats.

"Once I got friendly with a couple of guys who had a speedboat," he told me. "One day they invited me to take a ride.

"We went out to a larger steamer. There, they picked up two huge bags and put them in the speedboat. As we headed back to shore, they spotted a police boat following them. So they dropped the bags in the water and returned to the dock.

"I later learned there were Chinese men in the bags. They were smuggling them in."

Henny had witnessed a double murder. So much for the joys of the ocean air.

The sea had a lot of meaning to many Brooklyn natives. To health columnist Jane Brody, it was the wonders of science and nature at Manhattan Beach that first piqued her interest in health topics.

She would spend hours on her porch, playing with sea

creatures she had collected. She enjoyed the exercise and fitness the sea environment provided her.

Likewise, Elizabeth Holtzman, New York City's comptroller, has wonderful memories of ferry boat rides from Sheepshead Bay to Rockaway, on which, for a modest price, an entire day's recreation could be carved out of just the voyage, back and forth.

Editor Ralph Ginzberg recalls the days when Brooklyn's port and harbor were of much more importance to the city. He talks of New Year's Eve celebrations by the docks when the freighters would create a thunderous roar at the stroke of midnight, which added to the neighborhood revelry.

As I liked and admired Herbie's father, so did Herbie like my mother. He saw her goodness, and she saw him as a mature, good influence on me. Herbie was very mature in adult relationships. My mother would discuss my upbringing with Herbie when he was twelve or thirteen. So we were connected, we were almost family. Herbie's father was a realist. He was much closer to being an agnostic than to being a Jew. He thought most of the stuff Rabbi Morgenstern was dishing out in his sermons was propaganda. But often he would simply take an opposing view for the sake of a good debate. For example, when Israel was declared a state in 1948, Jews throughout Brooklyn celebrated. Morris took the minority view, just to start up. "Hey, the Arabs aren't such bad guys," he'd announce, and boom, a big fight. He took a fatherly interest in my dreams of being a radio announcer, and, standing outside George Richland's clothing store on 86th Street one day, said, "Radio, schmadio, are you kidding? Get a job, make a living, make something of yourself." I didn't go to too many people for advice, and, obviously, I didn't take Morris Cohen's that day, but I could listen to him without being offended.

When I made it in radio, while there were some I would have liked to say, "Told you so," to, Morris wasn't among them. He was proud of me, and I was pleased to make him proud, just as my father would have been.

FOUR

WARRIORS

THERE WEREN'T ANY street gangs, as we think of that term today, in Bensonhurst. There were some tougher gangs in my old neighborhood, East New York, but crime seemed to be the province of hoodlums, acting individually. We didn't know the term *mugging*, but we knew of stickups and holdups, and occasionally, big-time crime that would hit the front pages of the *Daily News* and the *Daily Mirror* and have everyone talking for weeks. Some of us cut out the "Crime Stoppers" tips from Dick Tracy in the *Sunday News*.

Louis "Lepke" Buchalter was our hometown hood made good. The Brooklyn-based gangster, whose "Murder Inc." lent itself to the stuff of legend, was at his peak in the thirties, but his reputation, with the unusual twist of his being Jewish, made him larger than life. That he eventually fried in the electric chair in Sing Sing, "up the river" in Ossining, New York, made the story all the more fascinating.

One of the most intriguing moments in Lepke's career came in 1941, when he was on trial for murder. A key witness, Abe "Kid Twist" Reles, was being protected at the

Half Moon Hotel on the Coney Island Boardwalk. Five policemen were assigned to protect him in his sixth-floor
room. Reles was a Jewish mobster, prepared to squeal on his
former buddies from Murder Inc.

With all five cops claiming to have fallen asleep, Reles
was removed as a witness when his body was found lying on
the roof of the hotel's kitchen, five stories below. He'd gone
out the window. The Half Moon Hotel would become a
tourist landmark and the source of years of speculation. Fifty
years after Kid Twist's mysterious death, no one was closer
to knowing the truth. The Half Moon was by then a senior
citizens center, the Metropolitan Jewish Geriatric Center,
scheduled for demolition.

Another Brooklyn hoodlum of renown was Albert Ana-
stasia, who was gunned down in a barber's chair at the Park
Sheraton Hotel in Manhattan in 1957 during a dispute with
Meyer Lansky's people.

Eli Wallach, who was born in the Red Hook section of
Brooklyn, "Little Italy," recounted this story for me one day:

"Many years ago I was asked to play Albert Anastasia on
TV, the Mafia boss who got knocked off in the Park Sheraton
barber shop. It was difficult for me to capture his essence.
Leonard Lyons, the Broadway columnist, suggested I spend
an afternoon with Judge Sam Leibowitz at Brooklyn
Supreme Court. 'He defended Anastasia on two murder
charges,' said Lyons. 'He'll tell you all about Albert.' So I
spent a day on the bench, sitting next to the august judge,
and learned nothing of Albert, but I could play tough Sam.

"Off I went to Los Angeles to shoot the show. There, the
producers suggested I watch a tape of Al's brother Tony
being questioned by the Kefauver Crime Commission. The
interrogator, in a high-pitched voice, said, 'And where do
you live, Mr. Anastasia?'

" 'I live-a one sixty-seven-a Union-a Street,' he answered.

" 'Turn off the tape,' I said. 'I was born at 166 Union!'

"Jewish or Italian, a neighborhood was a neighborhood. If you lived on the same block, you had the same life. And so I *knew* Anastasia and played him like he was my neighbor."

In 1947, a bunch of us formed a club called the Warriors. Don't let the name fool you. We didn't know from crime or gangland fights. We barely knew from Indians. We were a bunch of fourteen-year-old kids who thought it would be great to be joined together with a clubhouse and jackets, to partake in sports together, and to generally be there for each other. We had to pay fifty cents a week in dues for the general welfare of the club. We were not unique in the neighborhood; there were other social/athletic clubs as well. But I always thought the Warriors were special.

We got jackets, which were wool on one side, satin on the other, and it became a big decision to decide which side we would wear on a given day. The jackets were a major purchase, costing about $18 each. We had our names embroidered on both sides. The jackets were bright red, with white sleeves and white stripes on the wool side; exactly the reverse on the nylon satin side, with white buttons or red buttons, depending on which way we chose to wear them on a given day. It said WARRIORS on the back and our first names on the front. We thought of them as the most stylish things we had ever owned.

I saved my $18 delivering groceries. The day the jackets arrived was as big a day as I enjoyed in my teens. One of our members knew how to order jackets, and they were delivered to Bernie Horowitz's house, my friend we called Hoo-ha. Within minutes, word spread throughout the neighborhood that they had arrived. In a flash, we all rushed over, decided on wool side out, and strutted through the streets of Bensonhurst in our beautiful matching garments. I don't think I've ever had my chest out so proudly. Look out, here were the Warriors!

Bernie was known as Hoo-ha simply because one day someone said, "Hey Bernie," and he said, "Who?" In response, he was told, "What do you mean, 'Who?' I'm asking you something." And Bernie said, "Ha?" and was forever after Hoo-ha Horowitz. More than any of us, Hoo-ha had to be defined by his voice.

There was, in a Brooklyn manner of speaking, an aristocratic manner to the cadence of Hoo-ha's speech. He pronounced everything carefully, with a blend of Brooklyn, the South, the King's English, and a nasal intonation. Crazy Guggenheim, the old character created by comic Frank Fontaine on the Jackie Gleason shows from Miami, had the voice down pretty good, even though he never met Hoo-ha, and Hoo-ha was never drunk, as the Fontaine character was. He was one of the most memorable characters in Bensonhurst, and any story involving Hoo-ha dialect can only be fully appreciated by the memory of that distinct voice, something like, "Ma name is Buhnahdd Hohowitz, and ma friends call me Hoo-ha."

Years after the Warriors, Hoo-ha paid a visit to Herbie in Chicago. Both were now adults, married men with families. Hoo-ha rang the bell. The kids opened the door.

"Oh," said Hoo-ha, "yu must be Steven. Very nice to meet you. And you must be Richard. I figured that out by the process of elimination! Ha, ha, ho!"

Hoo-ha today defines himself as a successful manufacturer's representative. Delivering those three words is like molding it out of a lump of clay into a sentence. I wouldn't be surprised if his business card said "Bernard Horowitz, Successfulmanufacturer'srepresentative."

Hoo-ha was never in danger of being a Rhodes scholar, and Herbie and I would take advantage of this lovable aspect and have a lot of fun with it. For example, we would go to a foreign-language film, and Hoo-ha would sit between us. He wasn't fast enough to keep up with the subtitles, so we would explain the plot to him as he fell behind. Except we'd lie. We'd invent the plot just for Hoo-ha's benefit, making it as farfetched as we could. And Hoo-ha would say, "He killed his father? I don't remember that! What does that have to do with the Laundromat scene?"

Hoo-ha was probably our most valuable Warrior, for he provided us with our clubroom, the basement of his parents' house, down the street from Herbie on 85th Street.

We decorated the clubroom in an unusual way. We stole the furnishings. This was a Herbie concept, but somehow we didn't think of it so much as stealing as creative decorating.

We sighted a plush red sofa that would look great in the clubroom. It was in the lobby of an apartment building. Herbie's theory, then and now, is that if you act like you know what you're talking about, people believe.

Four of us dressed like delivery men. We walked into the building and told the security guard, "We're here to pick up a red couch for cleaning."

The guard would look confused, because no one had told him about this. But why would four guys show up to clean the couch if it wasn't arranged for?

So he'd point to the couch. Each of us would grab a corner. Herbie would ask the guard if he'd mind holding the door for us.

"Not at all," he'd say.

And out we'd go, walking down the street until we got to Hoo-ha's house. And we had our couch.

Yes, the security guard may have wondered where our truck was and why we were carrying this couch all the way down the street, but again, if you acted like you knew what you were doing, you might leave them scratching their heads, but you'd win.

One day Hoo-ha and I walked into a building and saw the most beautiful ashtray ever invented, sitting by the elevator. All of us smoked in the Warriors. We smoked terrible unfiltered cigarettes; Luckies and Old Golds and Chesterfields and Philip Morris, which was my brand of preference because that was what my father smoked. My mother never minded my smoking, but it was more acceptable among young people in those days, and there was little she could do to discourage it. It took my heart attack, thirty-five years later, to get me to stop. Anyway, this ashtray would be perfect for the clubroom.

It was an ashtray chained to the floor to protect it from theft by undesirables. It was silver and black and must have weighed thirty pounds. It was Hoo-ha who spotted it and said, "Oh, this would be great for the club!"

So the two of us brazenly walked over, yanked it out of the floor, chain and all, and carried it out of the building. We had to walk three blocks to Hoo-ha's. Two guys, carrying a thirty-pound ashtray, chain dangling below it, walking through the streets of Bensonhurst in broad daylight.

Suddenly, a cop comes by. We're face to face with him. He looks at us, but doesn't say a thing. He has to know that we've just pulled the caper of the afternoon. And Hoo-ha looks right at the cop, and says, "We like to keep our streets clean." The cop is laughing now. "We carry this around to put our cigarette butts in for a cleaner New York."

The cop knew. They always knew. But New York cops were great. They understood that certain things were just meant to happen, like two dumb kids stealing an ashtray, getting caught red-handed, and talking about cleaner streets.

Hoo-ha was never without a carefully delivered explanation for his exploits. One day we're all at Ebbets Field, that holiest of sacred temples in the borough of Brooklyn, to catch a Dodger game, and we decide the time is right to sneak into the reserved seats. Hoo-ha announces that he'd found an easy way to do it.

"Ah go over that gate right there," he says, "and make a right."

As much of a holy site as was Ebbets Field, the mystique of this wondrous arena did not put us in such awe that we were incapable of sneaking in or finding better seats. The only problem with Hoo-ha's theory was that he got stuck halfway up over the gate. He couldn't go forward, he couldn't go back. Meanwhile, having chosen a different path, the rest of us are already in the reserved section, waiting for Hoo-ha. We see him, pinned by his stomach, his top half in the reserves, his bottom in the unreserved section.

An usher came at last. We're all sitting there looking at our friend. The usher takes a look at Hoo-ha and says, "What the hell are you doing?"

And Hoo-ha, in as unlikely a position as you'd ever want to be found, simply says, "This is the way I like to watch ma baseball."

Hoo-ha was removed to the unreserved section.

His explanation had its roots in our constant rationalization of bad situations. In Ebbets Field, you could get some of the worst seats in America. We'd have seats where you could barely see the sliver of the field between the people in front of you and the poles on your sides. And Hoo-ha would say something like, "I like to get a view of just the first baseman's head on occasion. You can learn a lot about the game this way."

Or you'd be way out in right field, barely able to tell who was at bat, and one of us would say, "It's good to see the game from the right fielder's perspective now and then."

The clubroom, being in the basement, had high windows from which you could peer out onto Hoo-ha's driveway. We all had keys to enter the room, and the Horowitzes had very few rules of conduct for us. They were great. They even let us paint a Warrior head in luminous paint on the floor. This was an especially good conversation starter when we had girls in the room. We would tell them about this Warrior head, which could only be seen when the lights were out. So we had our excuse to turn out the lights and have the girls in the dark room. The first female breast I ever touched was a result of that neat little light show.

In the Horowitz home lived Hoo-ha's grandmother, Booba. This was a woman who outlived every doctor who ever told her she had two weeks to live. She was indestructible, and one of the things that kept her indestructible was this odd treatment from some quack in Brooklyn, who told the Horowitzes that to aid Booba's circulation they would have to roll her around on the floor from time to time like a keg of beer.

Spending as much time in the Horowitz home as we did, we knew the family well, and the idiosyncrasies and oddities of human behavior didn't faze us a bit. Bernie lived with his older brother, Leon, his parents, Nathan and Dora, and his uncle and aunt. Booba was Dora's mother. Hearing her being rolled around upstairs became a normal part of our Warriors meetings. If we had a guest, we'd say, "Noise? What noise? Oh, that? That's Hoo-ha's grandmother rolling around."

They kept her circulation going until she hit a hundred and six, when she had the bad sense to pass away on the afternoon of New Year's Eve, 1950/51. While we believed this was at last great news to Hoo-ha's father, who we were convinced had married Dora only for Booba's inheritance (she was reputed to have a lot of money in the mattress), this severely threatened to put a major cramp in our big New Year's Eve party plans for that night, with the festivities scheduled, of course, for the clubroom downstairs.

New Year's Eve was more than a little special to us. While none of us were what might be considered lady killers, nor was serious dating a major function of Warrior days, New Year's Eve did require a great deal of thought on getting a date and planning a party.

Although this was his grandmother, Hoo-ha was as angry about this poor timing as any of us. "Booba did this deliberately," he said. "She could have died anytime. She was a hundred and six years old. She died to spoil our party."

Herbie, however, was not to be deterred. He went to the grieving Mrs. Horowitz and announced how saddened the Warriors were by this unexpected turn of events.

"We have decided," he said to Hoo-ha's mother, "that our little gathering this evening will be a celebration of the life of Booba. We are going to hang black crepe and dedicate New Year's Eve to Booba's memory!"

And that's exactly what we did. The Warriors' New Year's Eve Party was dedicated to Booba, although I'm not sure I heard her name mentioned all night.

Hoo-ha read in a magazine once that the idea of certain foods not "going together" was all mind over matter. The idea of not mixing things like pickles and ice cream was all false. "If you like pickles, and you like ice cream," the story said, "you should be able to eat them together. There's no medical reason why you shouldn't. It is mind over matter."

Hoo-ha was stuck on this mind-over-matter thing. For days, all he could talk about was "mind over matter, mind over matter."

"It makes a lot of sense to me," he'd say, in that aristocratic Brooklyn drone. "Ah like pickles. Ah like milk. Ah could eat pickles. Ah could drink milk. It's all mind over matter."

Herbie had finally had enough.

"Okay, Hoo-ha," he said, "here's the deal. I'll bet you ten dollars that we can go over to the Feedbox and put together a concoction of six foods you like. If you finish it, you win the ten dollars."

"All six I love?" said Hoo-ha.

"All six," said Herbie.

"You got a bet," said Hoo-ha. "It's just a question of mind over matter, mind over matter." So we went to the Feedbox on 86th Street, where they had a full menu. And Herbie tells the waiter, "Okay, bring us a platter of ice cream, baked beans — you like baked beans, right Hoo-ha? — scrambled eggs — okay, Hoo-ha? You like scrambled eggs? — pickles in chocolate syrup, and a glass of milk."

And Hoo-ha's already counting his $10. He's saying out loud, "I like pickles, I like ice cream, I like milk, I like chocolate syrup, I like scrambled eggs, and I liked baked beans! It's just mind over matter, mind over matter."

Hoo-ha took a seat, tucked a napkin under his shirt, and threw up about ninety seconds into the feast.

*   *   *

One day Hoo-ha proudly announced that he had completed a successful business transaction which could reap big profits. We arrived in the clubroom to find fifteen bricks neatly stacked. He told us someone had come by and offered him the bricks for only $3.

"Hoo-ha, what are you gonna do with fifteen bricks?"

"I don't know," he said, "but some day, someone is going to come by needing bricks, and when that day comes, I'm going to make a big profit."

So the fifteen bricks took their place with the ashtray and the couch in the clubroom.

The ugliest moment in Warrior history came one afternoon when Herbie and I coaxed two girls named Angela and Theresa back to the clubroom for what we considered to be an easy make-out session. That such an activity could be considered easy is perhaps an overstatement, as we lived at a time when sex wasn't hurled at you on every television commercial, in every movie, and every magazine. We didn't know that being in a constant state of heat would one day be considered normal in society. So we took our opportunities as they came, but did not waste precious years plotting our next conquests.

While Angela and Theresa seemed like the ultimate bad girls to haul into the clubroom (i.e., a chance for a French kiss), we were taken aback when Angela, my "date," announced that she needed "a little mood." I looked at Herbie and he returned my glance. We had never considered that mood had anything to do with this. I was the immediate-gratification type.

Ever the opportunist, I bid them all wait a moment while I scampered up the steps to Hoo-ha's room, snatched his radio, and returned with the proper mood.

I was just about to head down the steps when I had to pass through Dora Horowitz's kitchen. Hoo-ha's mother was an unexpected obstacle. She was a large woman, formidable in fact, at five four and a *zoftig* 180 pounds. She was not graceful. She was standing there in a housedress and apron, with a huge wooden bowl, grinding liver into chopped liver. The steel tool she used was both a chopper and a grinder, which looked like a small outboard motor.

"Where are you going with Bernie's radio?" she demanded.

"We gotta listen to the ball game, Dora," I said. Hoo-ha's parents were known by their first names to us, probably because of the familiarity of being in their basement so much. No one else in the neighborhood was anything but Mr. and Mrs. Cohen, Mr. and Mrs. Rubin, Mrs. Zeiger, etc.

Suddenly Dora heard the giggles of two girls in the clubroom. You couldn't put one past Dora at this point.

"You have girls down there!"

"Listen, Dora," I said, with a sternness that surprised even me. "Outta my way. I'm going downstairs."

"You are not taking Bernie's radio down there, and you will ask those girls to leave at once."

By now Herbie, unable to entertain both of these girls by himself, had come to the top of the steps to see what was amiss. He was shocked to see how I was talking to Dora.

Dora, still clutching her bowl of chopped liver, moved her body to block the door. And I, filled with a combination of rising passion and disbelief over this unplanned intrusion, gave her a body check that would have impressed the New York Rangers. It was intended to be a shove to clear my path. I felt the clubroom was ours, and the radio was Hoo-ha's, and this was none of Dora's business.

My body check on Dora resulted in her flying backward

across the kitchen. She lost her balance, hit the sink, and went down. The bowl of chopped liver went soaring in the air, some of it sticking to the ceiling, some of it scattered on the floor. Had there been a penalty box in the kitchen, I would have had five minutes. It was a tough hit, but a clean one, and Dora, probably shocked by my move, had either exaggerated her fall for effect, or was caught so completely dumbfounded that she took her fall legitimately.

Herbie stood there with his mouth agape. All I said was, "C'mon, we've got it," and thundered down the stairs.

Sad to say, my mission was a failure. I had taken too long. Angela and Theresa announced that the mood had been broken, and that they had to leave.

The story, however, didn't end there.

The next day, Herbie and I are standing on the corner at 85th and Bay Parkway. Herbie is leaning on the streetlight, and I'm in the middle of some story, when we see Hoo-ha coming down the block. He was walking with a stern determination, his fists clenched, obviously angry. It's the absolute truth that we had no idea what he was angry about. The Dora incident was completely forgotten by both Herbie and me, when we heard him, about twenty yards away, screaming "God damn you, Larry."

"Yesterday," announced Hoo-ha, smoke shooting from his ears, "you hit ma mother."

"What do you mean?" I said. "I never hit your mother."

"Yesterday," he continued, "at the clubroom door, you hit ma mother. Ma father is mad! We had no chopped liver for dinner. It was all over the floor and the ceiling."

"Hoo-ha, I didn't hit your mother. She was blocking the door and I tried to move her aside. I never hit her."

"Listen, Larry, how'd you like it if I hit your mother?"

"You gonna hit my mother?"

"How'd you like it if I kicked your mother in the stomach?"

"You gonna kick my mother in the stomach?" I was mad now. "You do that, and I'll come back and punch YOUR mother in the face."

"Oh yeah?" said Hoo-ha. "Punch ma mother in the face, and I'll take a bat and whack your mother so hard she'll be unconscious for three days. Four maybe!"

Herbie cannot believe what he's hearing. He is recoiling down the streetlight post on which he was leaning in uncontrolled laughter. Here were two tough Bensonhurst thugs in action, arguing over who could beat up whose mother. At the time, neither Hoo-ha nor I had any idea how funny this was. Herbie knew immediately that this would be a classic story for the ages.

I made peace with Hoo-ha, of course, and even made peace with Dora, who was a sweet, long-suffering woman, always gracious to us and really very fond of us. This was not always easy, especially when we were forever taking her mops, sticking them in the sewer and twisting off the mop heads for perfectly cut stickball bats.

Hoo-ha's father, Nathan, was a furrier, except it took us years to figure that out. He had some of Hoo-ha's speech patterns, and for years we knew he was something with f's and r's in it, something that sounded like a frrrer. Since we weren't all that interested in what the guy's parents did for a living, we just accepted that Nathan was a frrrer, waiting for Booba to die and get her inheritance.

Nathan's business being seasonal, he had a lot of downtime, and he liked to hang out in the clubroom with the guys. Sometimes he'd wander downstairs in search of a pinochle game, amazed to find the room empty. He couldn't imagine that we were all in school. He didn't think of us as kids. But when he could round up some guys for a game, he'd be there like one of the guys, saying, "Make trump, Davy," and playing for money.

Then there was Ben Rubin, or Benty, or Ben the Worrier. When I look at a photograph of him today, I can tell by the furrow on his brow that he's nervous about getting the photo done because he's getting too much sun. Benty would find the dark side of any situation and worry himself sick.

We had this English teacher, Mrs. Parker. She'd begin the class with the homework assignment.

"Before we begin," she'd say, "your homework tonight is to read pages one through eighty, and then answer questions one through five. Now, to today's lesson. Yes, Ben?"

"I'm just checking my notes, Mrs. Parker. Did you say read pages one through eighty and answer questions one through five?"

"Yes, Ben."

"Thank you."

Now it's forty minutes later. The bell rings, we're on our way out. Ben stays behind, goes to the desk, and checks again.

"Read one through eighty, answer questions one through five?"

"Yes, Ben."

"Thank you."

This was of course, too much for Herbie and me to resist. We'd wait in the hall and let Ben meet up with us. And Herbie would say to me, "Page one through ninety, answer questions six through ten, right, Larry?"

"Right, Herbie."

Ben would begin to sweat.

"No, guys, I checked," he'd say. "It's one to eighty, and questions one to five."

"That's not what I've got, Ben," I'd say.

"Me neither," said Herbie. I definitely wrote down one through ninety, six through ten."

So Ben would rush back to Mrs. Parker and check one more time.

Ben was especially valuable to have along whenever we went to Ebbets Field. No matter how sunny and cloudless was the sky, Ben would make sure he would hang on to all of our rainchecks, just in case. And sure enough, once in a while, we would get rained out before the fifth inning, and Ben would say, "No problem, guys, I've got all the rainchecks right here in my pocket."

Rain in the forecast? Ben had his umbrella, yellow rubber slicker, and black galoshes even if it was sunny in the morning. He would look after us like an I-told-you-so mom.

Years later, he was Bob Benton, making his living as a successful lounge singer in Colorado. He hears Herbie's in Vail, and he calls to say hello.

Herbie says "Benty, come on over for a visit. I've got a beautiful condo here." They agree to one o'clock.

It's one o'clock. Herbie's waiting outside. He hears the phone ring. It's Benty.

"Herbie, did you see the weather forecast?"

"No."

"Chance of snow. If I get caught in it, how will I get back? I've got to play tonight."

Visit canceled.

The story's not over.

The following summer, Herbie's back in town. He calls Ben the Worrier and invites him again.

No good. Sandslides. Ben's heard that there's a chance of sandslides on the mountains. He was working that night.

Herbie: "Ben, would you relax? You're a fifty-eight-year-old man!"

But he was forever Ben the Worrier.

We had a character in the neighborhood known as Second to Ben. That was his nickname, Second to Ben. His real name was Barry Rubin, and he had a crush on a girl named Frances Diamond.

Frances was an accordion player and met Ben the Worrier in a talent contest. Ben, despite all his worrying, was a helluva singer, and they started going together after the contest. *Really* going together, bordering on a scandal. They held hands in public. And, on occasion, Ben would have his hand around Frances's waist when they walked. Sometimes on her shoulder. This was not as bad as Carl Fisher giving his Warriors jacket to Sandy Andevelt, which was unthinkable, and somehow made the jacket impure, but in the scheme of things, Ben's hand on Frances's waist was a big scandal, and it drove Barry Rubin nuts.

One day, Barry could take it no longer. He went to Ben and confessed his deep and lasting love for Frances.

"Are you sure you love her?" he asked Ben. Ben said he did.

"Well," said Barry, facing up to the situation, "if perchance you should ever stop loving her, is there a possibility that I might be able to go with her?"

This seemed reasonable to Ben. No matter that Frances the accordion player had no say in this. And so Barry would inherit Frances and would be forever known as Second to Ben.

Neither one ever married Frances.

The Benson Theater, our neighborhood movie, didn't have the first-run films that they had in Manhattan, so they would forever hold raffles to boost attendance. Hoo-ha, Ben the Worrier, and I went one day. By chance, so, too, did our mothers.

Since we never won, Hoo-ha and Ben decided, what the hell, let's trade tickets. So they swapped their raffle tickets in an effort to change their luck.

The movie ended, the lights came up, and the manager of the theater went onto the stage for the drawing. He was surrounded by all these fantastic prizes, with the bicycles seemingly the best thing. There was clothing, sports equipment, a set of encyclopedias, toys, radios, all sorts of wonderful items. The deal was, you hold the winning number, you choose anything you want.

And so the manager reaches into the drum, and he announces Hoo-ha's number.

"My God," he said, "I WIN! I WIN! I WIN!" It was the first thing he'd ever won in his life. "MA DREAMS HAVE COME TRUE! I'M TAKING THE BASEBALL GLOVE!"

Now you have several problems. First, Hoo-ha's mother, Dora, can't believe he's going to take the baseball glove. Her choice would have been a suit of clothes, but at the very least, a new Schwinn bike certainly seemed like the best thing. The glove was one of the lowest-priced gifts. It wasn't even a Spalding or a Wilson or a Rawlings, it was some pancake model without a known label.

"Take the bike, take the clothes," Dora is yelling as they run up to the stage.

Ben the Worrier, of course, is part of the act, too. It had been his ticket. He and Hoo-ha swapped. Never minding the judicial precedents to this, Ben, in a fit of logic, says, "Hey, it's my ticket, he was just holding it for me."

So Ben runs up to the stage, and I run up, too, just for the hell of it. I saw a great drama unfolding and I wanted a front-row seat.

So now the poor manager of the theater is surrounded by Hoo-ha, saying, "MA DREAM HAS COME TRUE, I WANT THE BASEBALL GLOVE," Dora shouting, "The bike, the bike, take the bike," and Ben saying, "It's my ticket." From the audience, Ben's mother is yelling, "Don't shout, you'll have a heart attack."

Everyone in the audience is into this. "Take the bike," they're all yelling.

Hoo-ha took the glove. And for years thereafter, every time we'd play a game and Hoo-ha would wear it, Ben the Worrier would say, "That's my glove, you know."

We had Fonzie in our neighborhood long before Henry Winkler ever created the role on the hit series "Happy Days." Our Fonzie was Bucko, Sy Buckwalter, hair slicked back, very much into chicks, or as he called them, chi-wicks.

Bucko was not especially into sports, as they would mess up his hair, but one day when we were about seventeen, we found ourselves a player short to compete in an important game at the Jewish Community House, the JCH, or just "the J," where we played basketball. You needed twelve players on the roster, and you had to have eight suited up. The Warriors only had seven, so we recruited Bucko to sit on the bench and avoid the forfeit.

As Bucko worked out with weights, it was very difficult to get him into a properly fitting uniform. As he was getting dressed, he asked, "How do I look, will the chi-wicks like this look?"

Sure enough, they liked it. Bucko is sitting on the folding chair on the side, and he points out that "the chi-wicks are all looking at me, check it out, the chi-wicks are in love with me. They all like me."

He was right. They were all looking at Bucko.

Just as halftime was approaching, Inky Kaplan made a shot, and as he passed our bench on his way downcourt, he yelled, "Hey, Bucko, your nuts are hanging out. You forgot your jock."

We all had nicknames. Hoo-ha and Ben the Worrier you know about. Herbie was Handsomebo because one day he announced that he thought he was pretty good-looking. I was Zeke, off Zeiger, and sometimes Zeke the Greek, only because it sounded right. Funny thing was, I pronounced my name ZEEger, and my brother called himself ZIger. So it would be, "Hi, I'm Larry ZEEger, and this is my brother, Marty ZIger."

Inky got his nickname because he once drank a bottle of ink at his school desk, answering a dare from a teacher. His teacher had said, "Mr. Kaplan, apologize to the class for what you have done" (whatever it was), and Irving said, "I would sooner drink this bottle of ink than apologize." It took a good two years for all of the ink to wear off.

Inky later became a dentist.

There were guys who weren't Warriors but who played at the J, hung out at The Corner, and went to Lafayette High School. Some were better friends than others, but we knew them all. Sandy Koufax was one example. Fred Wilpon, who washed dishes at a Chinese restaurant after school, was another. They both played baseball at Lafayette, where Fred was a bigger star and went on to become half owner of the New York Mets. He pitched, and Sandy played first base, even though Sandy couldn't hit much. Sam DeLuca was a neighborhood guy who went on to play pro football for the Jets. Peter Max, the great pop artist, was no athlete, but he was a Bensonhurst guy by way of Germany and Israel. Larry Merchant, the boxing commentator and columnist, went to Lafayette. So did Gary David Goldberg, who created "Family Ties" and "Brooklyn Bridge."

Koufax was two years younger than me. He was born Sandy Braun, in Borough Park, but his parents divorced when he was three, and his mother married an Irving Koufax and moved to Rockville Centre on Long Island. Not many people were doing that in the thirties, and for that matter, we didn't know many people who came from divorced parents.

The day he graduated ninth grade, in the fall of 1949, Sandy and his family returned to Brooklyn, moving into a project alongside the Belt, a three-story red brick garden apartment. We never called it the Belt Parkway, just the Belt.

Basketball was Sandy's game. Because he was not a good hitter, he was never considered a baseball star, let alone a major-league prospect. His name, however, inspired awe among basketball devotees, for he had the moves of an NBA prospect, was a deadly shot, and an outstanding ball handler. But as a baseball player, he couldn't hit, not in Brooklyn and not in the majors, so he wasn't taken seriously as a baseball prospect, at least not until he found his niche on the pitcher's mound. He was a first baseman who couldn't hit in the years we knew him, and that didn't add up to very much. (His lifetime batting average in the majors was under .100.)

He was a familiar sight at the J, playing three-on-three basketball. There he'd play against East Flatbush and face guys who went to Tilden High, or against Brownsville and face Jefferson High kids. When a high school coaches' strike cut down basketball season at Lafayette, Sandy showed his skills at the J, taking his team to the finals against Worcester, Massachusetts, in the National Jewish Welfare Board championships.

When the strike ended and high school play resumed, in 1950-51, Frank Rabinowitz was the Lafayette coach. Sandy starred as a junior and was named captain in his senior year, when he scored 165 points in ten games, second in the conference. He was named All-City.

One day, the Police Athletic League, which did great things for all of us kids, arranged for a few of the New York Knicks to play a benefit game at the Lafayette gym. Harry Gallatin, Carl Braun, and Al McGuire were among the Knicks to make the trip out to Brooklyn. Sandy made a big impression on Gallatin that day, and it helped him earn a scholarship to the University of Cincinnati.

There he broke the freshman scoring record. In the summer, he was pitching in the Bay Ridge-Prospect Park League and playing an occasional first base. He threw hard, but no one had any idea where his pitches were going. Still, with that kind of speed, the Brooklyn Dodgers were willing to take a chance. He was signed by scout Al Campanis, who gained fame thirty-three years later by telling Ted Koppel on "Nightline" that blacks lacked the "necessities" for front-office jobs. Sandy insisted on a $20,000 bonus, both because his stepfather needed the money and because it was over the bonus limit and forced the Dodgers to keep him in the majors. Sandy figured he could still play basketball on the side, and when his class graduated, he would still be eligible to go into the NBA if baseball didn't work out.

When he was forced to stay on the Dodgers' roster, they had to cut another pitcher. That was Tom Lasorda, now the Dodgers' longtime manager. And we had our first-ever neighborhood guy in the big leagues.

Sandy was sort of a loner, as his later reputation bore out. He kept pretty much to himself, as he does today. Little did we realize the heights to which he would climb in major league baseball. Many people today will say he was the greatest player, never mind pitcher, of the last thirty years. It was said that he was simply playing a different game from everyone else when he stood on the mound. His fastball not only overpowered hitters, but it had a natural rise to it, making it a breaking fastball that rode up and away from hitters. His curveball was deadly, and left hitters swinging at the sound of it as it dropped. As fans measure baseball accomplishments by statistics, Sandy's, over a six-year period, remain awesome to this day.

Sandy retired on top in 1966, his arm facing crippling injury if he didn't quit. When you go out with a Cy Young Award and a world championship, with five consecutive earned run average titles, your legacy is intact. He has kept far from the spotlight ever since, but his name inspires awe among sports fans, as well as among those of us who knew him before he conquered the nation.

One day on The Corner, we got into a little show-off of strength. The idea was to lift the bus stop sign, which in those days was not stationary but rested on the sidewalk in a concrete base which weighed it down. You really couldn't lift this like a barbell because it was so heavy on the bottom end, but one day we had a weightlifting contest to see who could hoist it up the most times. There were grunts and groans from the best of us, especially Bucko, who did five. Sam DeLuca did, I think, six. Nick DeCicco, a star football player, did four. Lenny Lefkowitz, another Lafayette football hero, maybe four.

Sandy lifted it ten times, then put it down and quietly walked away. No one had really given him credit for that much strength, as he was slim and not very tall. He impressed us all very much that day. Seeing was believing, as major league baseball players would discover not too many years later.

Although my brother Marty was four years younger than me, I managed to have him made an honorary Warrior, jacket and all. He was selected to be our mascot. Until he received this honor, I had not paid that much attention to him. The age difference was a big one, even though we were roommates. We were not Big Brother/Little Brother who shared advice and stories. We had our own friends, our own lives. But now Marty fit in a little better, and I began to take greater pride in him, defending his loyalty to the Cardinals (even though it made no sense to me), and making sure he got his fair share of benefits from being a Warrior, mostly the pride and friendship that the jacket represented, as well as the sports competition at the J. I even rooted for the Cardinals when they weren't facing the Dodgers, just to support my brother. And I took him to Ebbets Field sometimes.

We could have fun together — I was Batman, he was Robin, we had costumes, and we'd roll around on the floor together — but on the streets, we went our separate ways. Once he got a crew cut and he looked so German that the guys started to call him Otto and I joined them in the teasing. But deep down I was embarrassed for him, and I suppose that is what is meant by blood being thicker than water.

Marty was a much more responsible person than I, and a better student, and maybe I resented those things in him. He never got into trouble. He saved his money; I didn't. He'd count his coins and hide them. I couldn't spend them fast enough. I stole a quarter from him once and he knew it, and he hated me for that for a long time.

But whereas I had experienced life with a father, he had been too young, and he was essentially raised fatherless. He was only six when dad died.

Marty had to perform heroic services for me one day when I had an illness that required penicillin. In those days, you only knew doctors from house calls. You never went to their office. And there was always blame associated with any illness: you didn't dress warm enough, you went outside with wet hair, you didn't wear a raincoat and galoshes. Part of this was fueled by the polio epidemic, which was damn scary. Paranoia set in quickly. Stay out of public swimming pools, avoid crowds, don't stand in a draft, watch what you eat. Everything required a reason.

Dr. Isadore Sackadorf of Eastern Parkway was our general practitioner, the man who operated on my mastoid infection. He was a hands-on doctor of the past, and he would charge you the usual $3 for a visit. Whenever Dr. Sackadorf paid a house call, I felt better immediately.

One time, it didn't work that way. I was sick and he prescribed the new wonder drug, penicillin. This was the big replacement for sulfa, the previous all-purpose cure-all.

The way you know that you're allergic to penicillin is that in about two hours, you start to itch. For me, it was in the groin area, on my fingers, all over. I was in trouble. Dr.

Sackadorf came back and said I was having an allergic reaction to the penicillin.

To rectify this, it was necessary to strap me down so that
I wouldn't scratch myself to death. And I needed cold compresses applied to relieve the itching.

"Whatever you do," said Dr. Sackadorf to Marty and my
mother, "don't let him scratch, and don't you scratch him."

Marty was trying to sleep, and all night long I was in
agony, tied to my bed, my mother bringing in cold compresses. I'm cursing penicillin, cursing Dr. Sackadorf, and
fighting the fierce itching. And I'm begging Marty to come
over and scratch me. Like the guy in the western movies,
begging his captors to shoot him. "Scratch me, please,
scratch me." Marty loved it. He wouldn't scratch.

I survived. My mother stayed up for twenty-four hours
with the cold compresses, and finally, some antihistamines
that Dr. Sackadorf prescribed did the job. Whether Marty
was just being obedient, or enjoying my suffering, I can't say.
But when I think of that torture, I can still see him on his
side of the room, his Cardinal pictures on the wall, doing
nothing and pretending to sleep.

And so I'd call out for Marty Marion or Stan Musial or Red
Schoendienst or any of those Cardinal players to help me
until Marty couldn't control a laugh, and then I knew he was
up and I could resume pestering him for help.

The local dentist, used by one and all in Bensonhurst, was
Jerry Sauer's father, Dr. Sauer. Dr. Sauer, known as Dr. Saw-
yer by his wife for some reason, enjoyed our pain. Dentists
in the 1950s had to enjoy pain, or there was no point to
being a dentist, except for the monetary rewards.

Dentists' offices were designed to intentionally frighten
you. The gloomy waiting rooms with stern-looking recep-

tionists invited you to bide your time awaiting your call. Behind closed doors, you would hear the gurgling gasps of patients, and the whirling buzz of the slow drills. The offices themselves were done in a funerel black. All the equipment was black and foreboding. The sound of the equipment was haunting; when the drill touched your tooth, sparks flew and the noise was fearsome. You'd see small pieces of tooth fly out. The dentist's implements looked like instruments of torture. There were no hygienists, no Star Trek–like lounges to relax upon. Everything was utilitarian and frightening. A bright light shone in your eye high above the trays and tools.

One day Dr. Sauer had Herbie sit in his chair. As he began to work, he calmly told Herbie, "Look, this is going to hurt. More than a little. If the pain becomes too overbearing, too excruciating, raise your right hand and I'll stop. Then you can rinse, rest, and we can continue."

Herbie had a pretty good pain threshold. You didn't take Novacain in those days because the shot was so painful, you'd do anything to avoid it. And, he didn't want to appear to be too wimpy. So Dr. Sauer began drilling. At nine seconds, the pain was not to be believed. But Herbie hung in there. Onward to thirty seconds, forty, fifty. Still, Herbie was a martyr.

At a minute, he could stand it no longer. Firmly, he lifted his right hand shoulder high and gave a stern "Halt" sign.

And Dr. Sauer said, "Heil Hitler!" and kept drilling. He was not only a wonderful dentist, but a master comedian.

My dentist was a relative on 14th Street in Manhattan named Dr. Dinhoffer, with an office not far from Busch Opticians. He also thought pain was good for you, but he was also a dentist-chair philosopher who offered wise counsel at no extra charge. One time I was in his chair, and apparently he had heard that I had a growing reputation for chasing girls. This was not really true, for we were all awkward in this matter, but I kind of enjoyed hearing him say that I had this reputation. Then he gave me some advice.

"Label, Label, Label," he would tell me as he prepped me for my drilling. "When below your pants dominates above the pants, you're in trouble. You, Label, are operating below your pants."

Dr. Dinhoffer was a wise man. He was right. He didn't change me, but he was right.

Toby Goodheart had black hair, round green eyes, a sexy little overbite, a nice body, and was, to me, very, very pretty. I put her on a pedestal and worshipped her. She was my first pain and suffering. I wrote "Larry and Toby," "Toby and Larry," on all my school books.

I would kill for Toby. She drove me crazy, but I loved her deeply. Her father was Max Goodheart, maybe America's only Jewish truck driver. Her parents wanted us to get married. My mother thought I could do better than the daughter of a truck driver. Pretty snobby attitude for Bensonhurst.

Toby lived at 1976 76th Street, which put her in New Utrecht High, not Lafayette. At night, I would go to her house and sit on the porch and look at her lovingly. Her folks had a bungalow in the Catskill Mountains, and I visited her on weekends. One day her parents went off swimming. And I had my first sexual experience that involved love.

I had lost my virginity sometime earlier, when six of us trekked off to the city to seek out a prostitute. We found a classic one, one with a golden heart.

One of us, who shall remain nameless, climaxed about ninety seconds into the experience, barely into the beginnings of foreplay. I think it was right after the what's-your-name portion of foreplay. Understanding how embarrassing this would be in front of the other five, this wonderful girl permitted this nameless innocent to stay in the room a full forty minutes — ten minutes longer than permitted — allowing for a second, and this time successful, attempt, as well as the plaudits of friends, who were amazed at the virility that required a forty-minute session.

Toby was the girl who wore a white cotton dress and accompanied me to a rare box seat at Ebbets Field. There was nothing I wouldn't do for Toby, and nobody could break my heart as easily as she could. One day I was at the J and Toby came in with Jerry Myers, a very good-looking basketball player. It was the most jealous moment of my life.

I talked about marrying Toby all the time, but she always said no, we were only seventeen, and eventually, we did go our separate ways.

Ten years later, I was broadcasting at Surfside 6, in Miami Beach. Now I'm Larry King, and I'm in the newspapers, and had even begun doing television work. The phone rings. It's Toby. She's now Toby Weinstein, married to Dr. Weinstein. Two kids, one four, one three. She heard me on the radio. Could they come by and say hello, maybe see the show?

My heart skipped four beats. My show was on at nine. I got there a half-hour early and said to my producer, "An old girlfriend of mine is coming over with her husband and two kids." And I was stammering when I said it. I was nervous. Toby was stirring up old feelings. To tell the truth, I don't think a week had gone by when I hadn't thought of her. I knew she would walk in the door and look exactly as pretty as I remembered her.

The door opened. She looked exactly the same.

"Larrrry, hello Larrrry, long time no see, Larrrry. It's nice to see you, Larrrry, this is my husband, Irving, Irving, say hello to Larrrry, we used to date, and this is my son, Sheldon, Sheldon, say hello to Mr. Zeiger from Brooklyn, and this is little Mindy, Mindy, shake hands with Mr. Zeiger, Larrrry, remember in the mountains? Irving, go have some coffee, Larry and I have to talk. Larrrry, how good to see you."

I'm saying to myself, "Get me outta here." It was incredible. She never shut up.

"Larrrry, your success, we're so proud of you."

And I'm saying to myself, "I was going to kill for this!" The producer was looking at me, and I'm thinking, "What happened to Toby Goodheart?"

The nice thing is, I still think about Toby. The seventeen-year-old Toby.

Woody Allen's first love came when he was in the sixth grade in Brooklyn. She, too, had a very sexy overbite. There was something about it — "the way she could bite into a slice of bread, eat the middle, and leave the crust" — that was exotic. Before the age of orthodonture, overbites were good.

One day, Woody went to great lengths to impress his sweetheart. He scouted out her favorite spot on the subway platform and boarded a train dressed as Superman. When the train arrived, doors opened, and out jumped Woody, right in front of his target. As impressive as this may have been, the effect was lost when the subway doors closed on his cape, and the moving train ripped off his costume. Sounds like a bit from a Woody movie? I swear he looked sincere when he told me this story.

Before there was Toby there was a girl named Sandy, who couldn't help but wear tight sweaters. To Sandy I owe my thanks for helping me realize that touching the real thing was infinitely better than admiring them in lingerie ads in the Sunday *New York Times.*

I had also developed a crush on one Goldie Markowitz, who looked an awful lot better than her name sounds. We had the beautiful shared experience of flunking the same subject together, which cast our fates in the hands of summer school. Like two star-crossed lovers, we traipsed off to the depths of despair, summer school at Lafayette High, while all the world rejoiced in the summer sunshine. Goldie had blue eyes and blonde hair, and like me, was not really dumb, just an underachiever. Her condition was temporary. Mine had seemingly become permanent since the day my father died. Perhaps this was why our love could only be temporary. She was out of my league, too physically mature, too much of a woman for a goofball kid like me.

I was always a leg man. Even before I knew I was a leg man I was a leg man. This can be traced to my cousin Loretta and to third grade and Mrs. Egghouse, who had a major league set of wheels. I know at that age I couldn't have understood what I liked about them, but I do remember being unable to keep my eyes off them when she would sit on her desk and speak to us. I would lean over the side of my little desk so the boy in front of me wouldn't block my view, and I would enjoy the scenery. I didn't know why I liked her legs, but I knew that I did. Mrs. Egghouse's legs were an inspiration, not a distraction.

But as Mrs. Egghouse was more or less a fantasy for me in third grade, so, too, were many of my teenage sexual conquests. We were just so dumb in this area, we never made it a high priority. I think Herbie had one girlfriend before he got married, a girl named Ruthie Levine.

Howard Cosell, probably the nation's most impactful sports reporter, lived at 329 Lincoln Place and described the first love of his life as being a beautiful, blonde eleven-year-old who lived on the same floor, but in the next apartment building.

"One night," he relates, "she was in her kitchen, and I was in ours, and the shades were open and we saw each other. We smiled. And then, for some reason, we began matching kitchen utensils through the window. I would hold up a pot and so would she. A knife. A fork. She'd match me. This went on for some time, until I finally got up my courage and blew her a good-night kiss. She returned it. I was in love.

"I would return to that window at the same time every night for the next two weeks. She never did. And I never had the courage to talk to her when I saw her on the street."

Cosell was one of us.

There was a seductive mystery woman that Herbie and I shared. It was one of the great sexcapades in the history of Bensonhurst. She was a fast-and-loose woman who was capable of handling two boyfriends concurrently; a dazzling, seductive brunette whose wily ways would torment, but ultimately fulfill, the sexual psyche of any male. She took us into dark, previously unexplored carnal adventures that left us satisfied but determined to learn more. She had alluring dark eyes, a Veronica Lake hairstyle, and a figure one could only dream about.

We could only dream about it because we only knew her from the neck up. We called her Miriam Glick, not a sexy name, but one that would play in Bensonhurst. Trust me, she didn't look like a Miriam Glick. She was the photo that came in the wallets Herbie and I bought. And we had a girl sign the photos to us, individually, with love. And we would say, "We're going to see Miriam now," and we'd disappear for a couple of hours.

The guys bought this. They really did. The name was important to make this work in Brooklyn. If we'd called her Kathy Russell, we wouldn't have put it over. No one named Cohen or Zeiger dated anyone named Kathy Russell of Bensonhurst.

As time went on, the mystery of Miriam Glick grew. Arnie Perlmutter would say, "Again? You guys are going to her house again? Wow!" Naty Turner would say, "When are we going to meet her? Why don't you bring her around?"

Hoo-ha was especially intrigued by this dazzling beauty handling two of us at once. His imagination was all over the place. And then one day Hoo-ha says, "Larry, it's time to take care of your friends."

But I explained, "Hoo-ha, this is deeper than that. You have to understand. This is like a three-way marriage."

And Hoo-ha said, "I understand, I understand." And Miriam lived on in our wallets.

One night, shortly after I had started smoking, Hoo-ha, Herbie, and I went out on a triple date with three real girls. They all lived on the same block. My girl, Judy, was in the middle of the block, Herbie's on one end, and Hoo-ha's on the other. We went to a movie, then got some ice cream at Howard Johnson's. At the end of the evening, we all walked our dates home individually, and then we were to meet in the middle and compare notes.

Herbie goes one way with his girl, Hoo-ha the other with his, and I'm in the middle of the block with Judy. I had a cigarette dangling out of the side of my mouth, trying my best to look like Humphrey Bogart. Cigarettes were now a part of my life. I smoked when I showered, knowing just how to place the butt on the soap holder so it wouldn't get wet.

This was our first date, and you never kissed anyone on a first date. I think this was carved in stone on the Kings County Courthouse, with a special emphasis on Jewish girls. Judy walked with me to the top of her stoop, and then turned around. I'm about to say good night when, to my shock and amazement, she puckers up for a kiss.

I couldn't believe this. This just wasn't done. So in my shock, I kissed her back. I never removed the cigarette. I burned her right on her lower lip.

She let out a scream that caused lights to turn on up and down the block. Herbie and Hoo-ha came running. Had I touched her breast? Fathered her child?

The cigarette had burned a hole in Judy's lip. I can still see her face, her eyeballs popping out of her head. I was in such a shock — we both were — that it took a few minutes to compose ourselves and deal with the medical emergency. What a screw-up. But this was the Warriors at their smoothest.

Not all our pals were Warriors; the JCH brought us together with great guys from other clubs. The football team was an especially close group, although none of us were football types. At least not contact football. We played a street game called Association Football. In other parts of America, guys were growing up with shoulder pads and helmets and playing with yard markers and sidelines. On the streets of Brooklyn, you made do with the dimensions God dealt you — only so much area on the street, sometimes parked cars creating obstacles, and yard lines designated by dented garbage cans placed at strategic points. None of us seemed destined for the NFL, but as it happened, something about Brooklyn street toughness lent itself towards a number of guys, once they had good coaching in high school, going on to play top-level college ball and even pro football.

Lenny Lefkowitz was especially close with the football guys. The Lafayette team was the city champion in 1952 under a very special coach, Harry Ostrow. Coach Ostrow was a very important figure in the neighborhood; his honor almost defined the standards we tried to keep. He was a former paratrooper, and his word was law. He had the respect of every student in the school. There was something about the way he carried himself, the confidence and dignity he portrayed. He was our Vince Lombardi. You'd run through a wall for him. If you weren't on the team, you probably had him in gym class, as I did. And he took no excuses in gym. You had a rope to climb, you climbed it. You never got out of anything, no matter how skilled you were at scheming up an excuse.

He came back for our thirty-fifth reunion a few years ago. He was ninety years old, and he went on the stage to speak. He said, "Quiet, please," and a hush fell over the entire room. People are going "Shhh, quiet, it's Mr. Ostrow." And the whole group honored him with a thunderous ovation.

I was the emcee. He came over to me and, in a very soft voice, said, "I watch you every night on TV." And I said, "Thanks, Mr. Ostrow."

I call a lot of congressmen by their first names. A lot of cabinet members. Under the right circumstances, I might one day say "Jerry" or "Jimmy" or "Ronnie" or "George" to you know who.

But Harry Ostrow was Mr. Ostrow to me.

Lenny tells a story of a particularly tough gang of kids from Bay 50th Street, rushing past Lafayette guys at The Corner and leading them to the J. Inside the J, the Bay 50th guys swooped inside and snatched a scrappy little guy named Mel Schreiber. They brought him out into the street to fight.

Mel is holding his own in a one-on-one fight, but then five more guys from Bay 50th jump in and start to pummel him. At this point, like the greatest Hollywood hero, Nick DeCicco, one of the best football players on Lafayette, jumped in for us. Nick was generally considered the best street fighter of all time. He went on to star at the University of Maryland when they were nationally ranked, and was one of the best-liked students both in high school and college. A big hero.

Nick jumps in, throws one punch, and two guys drop. He announces, "Okay, this is going to be one on one, and one on one only!" So one Bay 50th guy steps forward, and Mel clobbers him. Within seconds, the cops arrive and everyone leaves. DeCicco was the hero.

The feud with the Bay 50th guys was unusual. We had a lot of harmony among ourselves. We really never used the word "hate." The fact that we were Warriors and others were Pirates or Priams didn't matter. We competed hard on the basketball court, and lived in peace off it. We had no racial prejudices. Once, Coach Ostrow took out his star player and put a black player in. The star said, "The nigger is haunting me; I'm quitting." The entire team voted not to allow the star back onto the team until he had apologized to the black player, Coach Ostrow, and all of his teammates. He did.

FIVE

EDUCATING ZEIGER

BESIDES HAVING my mother dote on me more than ever after my father died, my teachers felt sorry for me. I always managed to find a way to let them know that my father was dead. If I didn't do my homework, my mother would come in and explain that "the boy doesn't have a father; he has to help me after school." From grade school, when he died, through high school, I was a student whose motivation had gone south.

So if I hated a subject, I didn't try, and I fell behind. Science would be an example. But if I had an affinity for a subject, like algebra with Mr. Feinman, I'd know it the first day and get A's and 100s all the way through. I either got it right away or relied on the sympathy of the teachers to struggle through. And it worked.

Herbie and I, close friends, truly became identified with each other for all time when we had our year-end talent show at JHS 128, Bensonhurst Junior High. That was the day we became Spark and Plug.

*   *   *

"In olde New York, in olde New York . . ."

That was the lyric that introduced our big talent extrav-
aganza. As I recall, most of the class was in the talent show,
leaving the parents and the few other kids as the audience.
The French teacher, Mr. Feldman of all people, was in
charge.

Neither Herbie nor I had any particular talent. We
couldn't sing or dance, we didn't play any musical instruments. Herbie could hum in class to cause a distraction, but
that wasn't the sort of talent you put on a stage. Mostly our
talent was in schmoozing, that is, story-telling, getting a
crowd to listen to us. We had minor parts in the show, and
our main function was to operate the curtains.

Now the dilemma for Mr. Feldman was what to do to
hold the audience during scene changes when the curtain
was closed. There was some thought of having Ben Rubin
go out and sing, but Ben Rubin was, and is, Ben the Worrier.
If there was anything that might go wrong, Ben would hone
in on it and worry. And he worried that he couldn't carry off
this solo performance, so we volunteered to handle the
intermissions.

My mother made hobo outfits for us on her sewing machine. Opening night arrived, the curtains closed, and out
we came from opposite sides.

"Hi, Spark," I said.

"Hi, Plug," Herbie answered. And we were off. Off with
the corniest jokes you'd ever heard.

"I know a joke about a chicken," said Spark.

"Oh, yeah?" I answered.

"But I don't think I'll pullet," he said.

"I'd duck if I were you!" I said.

"Oh, that was fowl!"

Awful. But, huge laughs.

"I'm a mechanic at Madison Square Garden."

"What does that mean?"

"I fix fights."

We brought the house down.

We were hits. There were five scenes, and we were the "fill" between each, and each time we went on we got bigger laughs and louder applause. We stole the show away from Ben, who was dying and who didn't talk to us for two months, and from Judy Brickhouse, the star soprano, who was hoping to be discovered that night. This was fine with me, because I hated Judy. She was an A student, and one day all of our grades were posted on the wall. Science, one of my worst subjects. I knew I'd failed, but I looked up and saw 66 and let out a great sigh of relief. Judy was standing there, reading over my shoulder. She got a 98. And she was crying and screaming out loud, "Where could I have gone wrong! What could I have done?" I nearly leveled her that day.

We were so big that in the grand finale, "Casey Would Waltz with the Strawberry Blonde," when the whole cast was on stage, Herbie and I, off in the back but still in our hobo costumes, got standing ovations as soon as we came out. I was dancing with a girl about six feet tall, and Herbie was dancing with someone much shorter than him. It looked like a continuation of our act. At one point, the choreography had us dancing near the front. We weren't taking a bow, we just happened to wind up there. The audience gave us an ovation right there in the middle of the number. The finale was essentially ruined; everyone was laughing just at our presence.

We toured with our act. Actually, the whole troupe did performances at other schools, but Spark and Plug remained the stars. Now I had my bar mitzvah speech and the Spark and Plug experience behind me. I had a sense that I could work a crowd real well. I could imagine myself captivating a radio audience. I'd fantasize about holding them through commercials and making the sponsors cry out for more. With each succeeding episode, I became more and more convinced that radio was my destiny.

It also put a glow around me because I was aware that my academic performance was falling off, and when I gave thought to that, I knew I was hurting my mother.

The Story of Moppo, like the telling of the Hebrews' exodus from Egypt each Passover, cries out for retelling. When I used to tell the story, I called Moppo "Melvin Goldfarb" to protect the innocent. Now the statute of limitations has passed, and no one was more innocent than poor Moppo. His real name was Gil Mermelstein.

We called him Moppo because of his wild curly hair. Moppo hung out with us but wasn't really part of our close circle of friends. The three rogues in the Moppo caper were Herbie, a guy named Brazzy Abate, and me.

We were in ninth grade, approaching our final weeks at Junior High School 128, with little on our minds except summer vacation and Lafayette High the following September. We had had undistinguished careers at 128 and were playing out the string.

When Moppo missed several days of school, the three of us walked over to his house to see what the problem was. There, sitting on his stoop, was Moppo's cousin, looking lonely and forlorn.

"A tragedy has struck us," he said. "Gil has come down with tuberculosis. His parents have taken him to Arizona for a cure, and I'm here to close up the house. Tomorrow I have to go to his school to tell them he's moved."

Herbie, ever our fastest thinker, moved into action.

"Listen," he said, "there's no reason to hang around for

that. We'll go to the office tomorrow and inform them of Gil's situation."

"Say, thanks a lot," said the Mermelstein cousin. "Now I just have to wait for the phone company to disconnect the phone, and I can leave."

So off we went to our corner. We could see that Herbie had a plan.

"Tomorrow," he began, "we go to Mrs. Dewar and tell her that Moppo died. She'll report it to the principal; he'll call Moppo's home to check it out, he'll find that the phone has been disconnected, and he'll cross Moppo's name off the graduation list.

"In the meantime, as Moppo's best friends, we'll go around and collect money for flowers for Moppo's family. If we can get fifty cents a kid, we can take in fifteen bucks and have the feast of our lives at Nathan's."

This sounded fine to Brazzy and me, although one of us did question what happens in the fall when Moppo comes back.

"Hey," said Herbie, "by then we'll be at Lafayette. No one will remember. And if they do, it'll be so long after this happened, no one will care. Fifteen bucks is fifteen bucks!"

And with that, the Moppo Caper of 1947 was born.

The next day we went to Mrs. Dewar in homeroom and told her that Moppo had died. Sure enough, she reported at once to Dr. Cohen, the principal. He called the Mermelstein home, discovered that the phone had been disconnected, and marked Moppo's card "deceased."

We collected our money for flowers and went out to break the all-time hot dog and knish record at Nathan's.

But that wasn't the end of the story.

Two weeks later, Mrs. Dewar told us that Dr. Cohen wanted to see the three of us in his office at once.

While Brazzy and I felt panic set in, Herbie whispered, "Don't worry, don't worry, we'll just say we had *heard* he died, and we're thrilled to know he's still alive. We'll say we sent the money to charity and we'll do our best to give it back."

Dr. Cohen was not upset, however. He welcomed us into his office and showed us three seats.

"Boys," he said, "I have some wonderful news. The junior high administrators in New York City have decided that high schools get too much attention in the newspapers because of their sports teams. We have convinced the *New York Times* to begin a series on worthy accomplishments in junior highs. And the *Times* has agreed that your efforts on behalf of Gil Mermelstein should be a feature story in the paper.

"So, we are going to establish a Gil Mermelstein Memorial Award. The outstanding graduate of JHS 128 each year will have his or her name placed on a permanent plaque, and we will have an award assembly before graduation. The *Times* will be here to cover it, and we want you three boys to present the first award."

Looking back, I would have to say that this would have been a good time to confess to our mischief and call the whole thing off. But something about the drama of the moment swept us away. We saw ourselves up on the stage, making this solemn presentation in Moppo's honor, getting our picture in the paper. So we said nothing. We knew we'd have the summer to get through it, and we could always explain in the fall. What were they going to do, put us back in junior high?

Two weeks before graduation, the assembly was held. All the seventh, eighth, and ninth graders crowded into the auditorium. There was a huge banner over the stage, "GIL

MERMELSTEIN MEMORIAL." The *Times* had sent a reporter and a photographer. We were on the stage with Dr. Cohen and the winner of the award.

At this moment, in what Herbie still describes as the finest moment of tubercular medical history, Moppo returns from Arizona. He has been cured in record time. He is late for his first day back in school, and when he arrives, he finds the classrooms empty. So he goes to the office, where they tell him that everyone is in the auditorium.

There are two ways into the auditorium — a side door, fairly inconspicuous, and the huge bronze doors in the rear that let in enough light when opened to play a night game at Ebbets Field. Moppo selected the bronze doors.

We had just finished the Pledge of Allegiance when Moppo entered. Those in the rear saw him first. Now even the dumbest of the dumb at 128 knew a scam when he saw one. Those who had contributed fifty cents for flowers were immediately pissed off. Those who hadn't knew at once they were about to witness one of the longest detentions ever dished out to three students in New York public school history.

Moppo took one look at the word "MEMORIAL" in the sign, and the three of us on the stage and figured the whole thing out. Laughter began to fill the room. The kid receiving the award panicked. Amidst the growing chaos we were hearing, "Do I still get the award? Do I still get the award?"

Herbie stood and shouted, "Moppo, go home. You're dead." And with that, Moppo turned and ran out through the bronze door amidst all the confusion, not to be seen again that day.

Dr. Cohen was not as quick as the rest of the kids to catch on because he didn't know Moppo, didn't recognize him, but in short order he figured things out.

He ordered the three of us into his office immediately, with the guys from the *Times* trailing rapidly behind. And all this while, while Brazzy is thinking that his medical career has ended, and I'm thinking that my mother will die from shock and I'll be an orphan, Herbie is whispering, "Don't worry, don't worry, I'll handle it, don't worry."

The essence of what Dr. Cohen had to say was something about detention, probation, expulsion, no graduation, no high school, criminal action, Riker's Island, lives ruined, and so on.

He hadn't even finished when Herbie interrupted.

"Wait a minute, Dr. Cohen, you're making a big mistake."

Dr. Cohen fell silent for a moment.

Herbie continued. "You're right, you've got us, we'll definitely be suspended, and we deserve it. But you've got to think ahead, Dr. Cohen, you've got to think about the consequences!

"When you suspend us, you'll have to file a report with the Board of Education. And they're going to conduct an investigation. And they're going to go back and find that you made one phone call, discovered the phone was disconnected, and marked the card 'deceased.' They're not going to be very proud of your work on that one, Dr. Cohen. This could end any chance you might have of advancing in this school system."

Dr. Cohen had to admit that Herbie had a point. This ninth grader had seen through the whole picture. Dr. Cohen was a beaten man.

We went out of his office and confronted the guys from the *Times*. They admitted that this was more a *Daily News* story, and agreed not to write anything.

Moppo never did understand all the subtleties of the

story, and that it was only about getting some loot to go to Nathan's.

There he stood along with us on graduation day, two weeks later, awaiting his junior high diploma. Dr. Cohen was reading off the names in a solemn manner. Herbie had already received his by the time they got to the letter *M*. When Dr. Cohen said, "Gilbert Mermelstein," Herbie rushed back to the podium, moved Moppo aside, and said, "I'll take it Dr. Cohen. Moppo's dead."

From the high we had as Spark and Plug and the great Moppo Caper we should have been rolling as we entered Lafayette High. But it being a very large New York City public high school, we felt a little disoriented. We were no longer big fish, as we saw ourselves in junior high.

Lafayette opened in 1939, an enormous and classically designed high school, born of President Roosevelt's Works Progress Administration. It was not yet a decade old when we entered, but no longer had a "new" smell or feeling. It was now more like a traditional institution of higher education, a public works project of five floors of concrete, with offices, a gym, and an auditorium downstairs, and then endless classrooms which could take many minutes to traverse between periods. It was an enormous place, home to nearly twenty-five hundred students, I suppose, and a faculty of nearly ninety.

Lafayette was a neighborhood school, with residential property across the street on one end, but then a large blacktop and baseball field on the other to create an openness which seemed alien to its surroundings. A lot of students went home each day for lunch. I don't remember much greenery, save for some plantings alongside the wire-mesh fencing which surrounded the blacktop. There was only a baseball field there, a field which saw Sandy Koufax and the Aspromonte brothers, Bob and Ken. The football team had to find other schools with open days on their schedules, like Lincoln or Erasmus Hall or Brooklyn Prep or Midwood.

The school, which became the setting for the "Welcome Back, Kotter" series on television (the series that launched John Travolta), has had an enormous success record with its graduates, many of whom have become prominent business and civic leaders, academicians, and financial giants. Among the graduates are singer Vic Damone, advertising genius Jerry Della Femina, TV producer Gary David Goldberg, economist Dr. Irwin Kellner, sportswriters Phil Pepe and Larry Merchant, Mets owner Fred Wilpon, artist Peter Max, actor Paul Sorvino, Federal District Judge John Sprizzo, and a bunch of guys with names like Bucko and Hoo-ha, Herbie and Larry.

At the end of our very first semester, Herbie and I found ourselves in the general program. The general program was mostly for disciplinary problems. It was the academic program that was for people with futures. This was a big blow to Herbie and me. We had been goof-offs, but deep down, we knew we were pretty bright. Now, Lafayette was telling us they didn't believe it.

For me, the reason was simple. I stopped doing homework. If I was good in a subject, I just got it and coasted. But if I had to work at it, I didn't. As a broadcaster, all I'm asked to do is perform. That, I can do. I've never had a problem with management in all my years on the air, because I can do what they ask. I've never been called on the carpet, dressed down, told to shape up, nothing like that at all. And I've won a Peabody, a Broadcaster of the Year, Ace Awards, many honors. And all because I do what I'm asked to do.

In school, however, where homework and study were necessary as an extra step, I wasn't prepared to take it. My brother would leave the light on and study and excel. I would pull the blanket over my head and go to sleep. There was no immediate gratification to homework. And I was always Immediate Gratification Zeiger, a forerunner to being Immediate Gratification King. It's why I love doing live radio and live television.

My brother was never out of work, never lost anything. I was always a victim of the easy-way-out philosophy if it didn't have a quick payoff. This worked for me in some ways, and against me in others. I always needed a happening, some quick action.

So for school, I was prepared to coast and take the consequences.

It was rougher for Herbie, who had an older sister who was an A student. In fact, she graduated college at eighteen. Herbie would come home with a C and tell his father it was for "commendation," but his sister would say, "Are you kidding? This is horrible! This is a disgrace!" So he couldn't bluff things at home with the sister looking over his shoulder.

Being in the general program embarrassed both of us, Herbie more so. We were walking to school one day (the school was at Benson Avenue and Bay 43rd Street), and Herbie looked at me quite solemnly and said, "Larry, this is not good. I feel like we're in the FBI — forever born ignorant."

It was true that we were treated like felons, and the period of our incarceration was spearheaded by our homeroom teacher, Mr. Starrs.

Mr. Starrs was about six feet tall, and like all of our teachers, he had no life, in our eyes, outside the classroom. We did not know anything about our teachers; where they lived, what religion they were, how they voted, whether they were married (unless they were Mrs.), whether they had children, how they got to school, whether they ever had sex, nothing. When I say that I never met any Protestants during my years in Brooklyn, I don't include teachers, because we had no idea and never gave it a thought. The fact that Herbie and our junior high principal, Mr. Cohen, had the same last name never even occurred to me. Mr. Cohen was without religion, without soul, as far as we were concerned.

Mr. Starrs, a self-consciously imposing figure, was dedicated to discipline. "You kids are juvenile delinquents," he would tell us. Our biggest crime to that point might have been chewing gum.

"You're not going anywhere. My job is to get you through school and to keep you out of jail." It sounded crazy, but this is what he thought. At first, he was frightening, but as we got more comfortable in our surroundings, we would begin to test his limits.

For instance, he was very punctual, and many of his rules reflected this. We had to be at our desks, pencils in place, at 8:30.

"When I walk in that door at eight-thirty," he would announce, "there are no exceptions. You are in your seats, pencils in place. And anyone arriving after eight-thirty is late and will be so recorded. And at eight forty-five, this door locks, and you will not be admitted at all. Those are the rules."

One day, we're at our desks, pencils in place, at 8:30. Mr. Starrs had not yet arrived. By 8:45, he was still a no-show. I looked at Herbie. We knew the rules. At 8:45, that door is locked and you are just not admitted.

So I got up and locked the door.

I returned to my seat, and there we sat, pencils in place. Mr. Starrs arrived about 9:00.

The doors in the classrooms were half glass. We heard the doorknob turn, and we could see Mr. Starrs at the window. We all sat there.

Now Mr. Starrs was banging on the door, rather ferociously, as I recall. The girls are saying, "Someone should open it." The boys are saying, "Hey, rules are rules." Mind you, not too many girls were taking the noble position, because these were girls in the general program as well.

We could see that Mr. Starrs was pretty mad. You know the scene in *The Graduate* where Anne Bancroft is yelling at Dustin Hoffman for showing up at Elaine's wedding, and you don't need dialogue to know she's cursing. That was Mr. Starrs.

It was about 9:15 that he returned with a janitor, who opened the door and let him in.

"Okay," he demanded, "who did this?"

He was pounding his fist in the air and all but preparing for the certain bloodbath to follow. But we all sat, and no one stepped forward to take credit for locking the door, least of all me.

He changed his tack. "All right, children, I understand what took place here. In fact," he continued, "I admire and respect the person who locked the door. He was just following the rules. I salute a respect for procedure. I would like to commend that person. If he would be good enough to raise his hand, I would like to shake it and say 'well done.' "

Anything for a compliment, about seventeen kids raised their hands. I wasn't among them.

"Well, for those of you responsible," he said, "I'm going to make a notation of this. Would someone go and distribute pieces of paper to the seventeen? I would like each of them to sign their names so that I may personally compliment you at a later time."

This I volunteered for. I enjoyed monitor assignments, like eraser clapping, and as I went around to get signatures, I was met by silence. No one was going to sign. So I signed for everyone.

Now Mr. Starrs said, "Larry, bring those sheets of paper up here."

Now he turned on us like a warden in a George Raft prison movie. "You little sons of bitches, I've got you now," he said.

"So, I see Herbert Cohen, and I see . . ." "Wait a minute," said Herbie, "I didn't sign anything. What do you mean I signed?" And the same was repeated for each of the seventeen. All correctly denied having signed.

"Well, who signed these?" he asked.

"LARRY," said the Gang of Seventeen.

And Mr. Starrs grabbed the seventeen pieces of paper, threw them in the air, and stormed out of the room.

But Mr. Starrs was our inspiration. He made us realize that we had to get out of the general program. And we cracked down on ourselves and studied and got good-enough grades to go into the academic program. And it taught us that if we really *had* to crack down, we could. We could be like POWs in the Second World War, escaping through cunning, even under the gestapo regimes of the Starrs of the world.

Danny Kaye played a lot of movie and television roles in which he got into innocent mischief. He told me he had a lot of practice for those roles while attending Jefferson High in Brooklyn. Jefferson was the school I would have attended had I remained in East New York.

"I was a nut case," he said. "A real problem. A constant disturbance in school. I finally got thrown out, and they told me I'd never amount to anything."

*   *   *

Sometimes, all the goofing off would catch up with us, and we'd feel terrible about it. And because we had growing reputations as cutups, even when we tried to be taken seriously, we failed.

Once we had to select a poem and recite it in class. Naturally, I did "Casey at the Bat." If I had to do a poem today at the CNN Christmas party, I'd still do "Casey at the Bat."

I did it well. A lot of dramatics and arm movements. But when I got to the part that says "and the score stood two to four," there was something about the way I said it that made everyone laugh. And I appreciated the laughter, and was more effective at that point than I might otherwise have been. I played to the laughter. It was unappreciated by Miss Truss.

Miss Truss, who put us through our paces, was big on giving zeroes. A familiar sound would be, "Mr. Zeiger, give yourself a zero." Or, "Herbert Cohen, give yourself a zero." It got so that the zeroes were impossible to dig out from. A hundred on an exam, averaged with seven or eight zeroes, gave you no hope for passing.

Fortunately, her system called for us to personally put the zero in her marking book. And Herbie and I figured out that we could make the action of *erasing* previous zeroes look like we were entering a new one. So each time we had to "give ourselves a zero," we actually subtracted one. This was only effective if you had several going in. And we did.

Our attendance was much better than you would expect of us. We had such a good time at Lafayette that there was really no reason to cut school. Oh, we might cut an occasional class or two, but we were never truants in the sense of skipping school, going to Coney Island, and having a truant officer on your tail.

I did, however, once get caught by Dean Grady cutting a

class. He saw me outside in the school yard during classes
and had me hauled into his office.

Maybe it was because I had such a comfortable relationship with cops when I was very little, but this sort of stuff
never intimidated me. I was never scared of being called
into the principal's office. I didn't want my mother to hear
about it, but on my own, I was fine.

In fact, on this particular day, I stood there and listened
to all that Dean Grady could dole out. I apologized and was
let loose with a warning.

The very next period, he looked out his window and saw
me shooting basketballs in the school yard again. I cut the
next class.

Dean Grady actually came to our house for dinner once.
This was very unusual, for, as I said, we couldn't imagine
teachers or administrators having a life away from the
school. But my mother invited Dean Grady over for a nice
Jewish meal. This was a scene, for Dean Joseph Grady was a
very stiff-collared, austere man.

My mother liked him, however, and invited him during
one of her visits to the school. He had never had a "Jewish
meal," he acknowledged, so he came for dinner.

He stayed for about an hour and a half; sat there with
Marty and me (my mother never sat down of course), and
had a wonderful time. But if bribery was a consideration
here, he didn't go for it, because within a few days, he
spotted me outside his window again, and I got hauled into
his office.

We had a Speaker's Bureau at school, and I fit comfortably
into that activity. I was good at it. We did drama readings,
famous speeches, and we would be the ones who might
introduce a special guest at an assembly. So I might be in

front of the whole school, and say, "Lafayette High School is pleased to present Fire Captain Seamus O'Garrity, who will speak to us this morning about the dangers of overloading electrical sockets. Captain O'Garrity," and I'd bow and wave him up to the podium. I would ham this up pretty good and try to get a hand for myself as I slipped out of sight with a little wave.

To this day, I love speaking in front of crowds, even more than working on radio or TV. Those feelings were born in the Speaker's Bureau at Lafayette.

English. Miss Druss. Very sexy. I like her a lot. Her boyfriends would sometimes come to class to wait for her, and we would think about them having sex.

One fine day we had oral book reports. A ten-minute oral report on the latest book we had read.

To me, reading meant comic books and *Sport* magazine. I didn't really read books, except for Frank Graham's biography of Lou Gehrig, *A Quiet Hero,* and John R. Tunis's baseball novel *The Kid from Tompkinsville.* But a report was a report.

So I got up and said, "Thank you, Miss Druss. The last book I read was a fascinating book: *The Ultimate Power,* a vivid and compelling story by Grant Stevenson.

"World War Two has ended. The victorious nations must now deal with the new world order. New nations have been formed. Vanquished nations have lost their influences. We have the coming of age of communist governments. The U.S. and Russia must work out a new relationship, having been allies during the war, but now philosophically opposed in manner of government.

"*The Ultimate Power* is a revealing look into the behind-the-scenes maneuverings of the world's leading powers as the global politics and policies are formed for the postwar era."

On and on I raved about this book. It was all rhetoric I was picking up from the daily newspapers.

And I finished, and Miss Druss says, "Well, Larry, I must say, that is a very thorough report, an excellent report."

And somebody in the class yelled out, "There's no such book, Miss Druss."

My cover had been blown by the fiend.

Poor Miss Druss. She was so embarrassed. I really felt more sorry for her, because she was so pretty, than I did for myself when she gave me an F. I could live with the F, which was for lying and embarrassing her, but I couldn't live with her thinking I was a shit. So I had to get to work on smoothing over that relationship, and I charmed her with the biggest apology I could muster until she forgave me.

And then I did a report on *The Ultimate Power,* by Grant Stevenson, the following year for a different teacher.

This time it was for Mrs. Mizner, the female Hitler, who was built like an army tank. She wore only black, had a bun on top of her head, no sense of humor, and I despised her with a passion beyond hate. If each grain of sand on a beach was one level of hate, I didn't have enough to cover my feelings for Mrs. Mizner. Not only was she miserable and nasty, but she hated Jews. If there was a Jewish name to pronounce — and there were plenty — she would slowly emphasize it. She would say "Jack R o s e n b l a t t," or "Leonard L e f k o w i t z," or Lawrence Z e i g e r," or "Benjamin H o r o w i t z." If it was John Grayson, bingo, she had the name in and out before you could say Jesus.

To this day, I am pleased to report that no one blew my cover, and I got away with *The Ultimate Power,* by Grant Stevenson, in Mrs. Mizner's class. Served her right.

Mr. Weinberg was our economics teacher. Dull subject. Economics wasn't very interesting then because it didn't have any practical application to our lives. We aspired to make $200 a week and, with luck, have enough in a passbook savings account to earn 3 percent interest. Any extra money would go not into stocks or bonds, but into a Christmas club, administered by our mothers, that might pay you $50 at the end of the year. I think even a scholar like Mr. Weinberg found it dull. He would give us long sections in our textbook to read silently, and when we'd steal a glance upward, we'd see him snoozing at his desk.

Although our expectations in the earnings area were never great, my expectations of needs were substantial. I never handled money well. My problems in Miami, which were quite serious, have been well documented. But my training for those screw-ups was established in my youth. I wanted to have what Herbie had, and sometimes it required $20 that I just didn't have. So I'd borrow it. And I couldn't repay it promptly. And I'd get into trouble.

I had a job, once, working at a place called the Silver Shield. It was a business that consolidated your debts. To hire me for this is like hiring a drunk to look after the wine cellar, but I had this job. The Silver Shield was eventually put out of business by the state attorney general for taking people's money but forgetting to consolidate their debts. But we didn't know this, we were just workers there.

One of the owners was Bert Lee. In addition, he was the voice of the New York Rangers hockey team, and he would get me free Ranger tickets.

If he got me two, I would go around the block and announce that I had four. I don't know why I did that, but I always had to make things better than they were, even if they were pretty good to begin with.

I'd get three other guys to go, and I'd wind up borrowing money to buy two extra tickets.

I suppose there was a need inside me to look good in front of my friends, but it always wound up costing me more than I could afford. It must have stemmed from my father being dead and feeling like the poor kid in the neighborhood.

I'm more conscious of these feelings now. Then, who would even give it a thought?

I let people know I was fatherless. It was almost like, "Hi, I'm Larry Zeiger and my father's dead." I knew sympathy was a human emotion that could be manipulated to my advantage. Herbie taught me about advantage; I used what was available to me.

It was not a very noble trait. But I used it, had my mother use it on my behalf, and took advantage of any edge that this misfortune in my life presented me with.

Our other school was "The Corner." This was where you learned what was *really* going on in the world.

Had I been alive in the first century, I would have wanted to live in Rome. My God, where else? Imagine being anywhere but Rome?

In the middle of the twentieth century, Brooklyn, New York, was, to our thinking, the center of the universe. And Bensonhurst was an awfully good place to experience it from. The Corner was to Bensonhurst what London is to England. And we owned it.

We didn't own it in a literal sense, not by deed, not by birthright. But we had no territorial war over it. We felt comfortable there, it beckoned us, it was Bali Ha'i. No gangs fought us for the rights. There was room for all, but we seemed to be the most frequent inhabitants. We knew its smell, its topography, felt its latitude and longitude. We knew its sound, busy and alive, punctuated frequently by the screech of the el above us. We knew the stores and their owners for a full block down on each of its four axes. We knew this was the place where we would learn of life, debate the issues of the day, argue and befriend, spell out dreams, and make our plans. "I'm goin' to The Corner" was our equivalent of a quorum call in the houses of Congress. There could be no greater lure than the call to the point in the northern hemisphere where 86th Street met Bay Parkway in the borough of Brooklyn, in the City of New York.

Isaac Asimov, who came from Decatur Street, relates these "Corners" to the lack of air conditioning or automobiles. That forced people out of hot apartments and off to gathering places. "People were everywhere, talking, laughing, gossiping, and the roadways were relatively empty," he said. "I would walk the neighborhood and daydream. And those daydreams became material for my later fiction."

It was on The Corner that I developed my skills as a storyteller. If I went to a basketball game and the game took two hours to play, I would take three hours to tell about it.

Such stories sometimes became legend. One day I went to Madison Square Garden for a high school game, and saw a player named Sihugo Green of Boys High. Great name. Star quality. And what a player. I was captivated by his game. Couldn't wait to get to The Corner and tell everyone about this guy.

So my Sihugo Green tales took the better part of an afternoon. And I was right about him; he went on to star at Duquesne University and then played ten years in the NBA, mostly with teams that aren't around anymore: the Rochester Royals, the St. Louis Hawks, the Cincinnati Royals, the Chicago Packers, the Baltimore Bullets, and in the end, the Boston Celtics. Turned out he was a helluva guy, too. But Sihugo Green died young. He had cancer and he passed away at forty-five in Pittsburgh. His death hit me hard; I felt he was my guy. I felt he was my discovery. A lot of people thought of me when he died.

Same for a guy named Henry Booker. He was another New York City high school star, except all he did was shoot. I'd watch him and then report back to the guys about the adventures of Booker, and I'd pronounce his name short and fast and clipped, so that it was "Booker this" and "Booker that," and I made him into a legend.

One story that took me most of the day to tell was my first appearance ever on radio. I was seventeen.

It was not unusual for me to subway downtown and sit in the audience of a radio show. I was a radio junkie, and I loved seeing in person that which I had heard on the air. Radio was actually wonderful theater. If it was a drama, the actors would stand by tall floor microphones, reading their lines and tossing their scripts onto the carpeted floors as each page concluded. They would cup their hands over their ears to better hear their own deliveries. In the back, a sound-effects man would be slamming doors, walking up stairs, ringing bells, whatever. I kind of liked the toss of the script to the carpet. There was an elegance to it.

In 1990, I actually got a chance to have that very experience. I was a special guest voice on the hit animated series "The Simpsons," one of the hottest shows on TV and one of the best written. I played myself, and sure enough, just like in old radio, we did our lines and then tossed the script to the floor. I don't think anyone in the room that day — not

Homer, Marge, Bart, Lisa, Maggie, or any of the gifted actors doing their lines appreciated this touch as much as I did.

A mention of San Antonio, Texas, was included among my lines in that episode. I was just throwing out a lot of scattered thoughts, much as I do in my *USA Today* column, and I just blurted out, "and if you're betting, I love the San Antonio Spurs this year." I later learned that they played the bit over and over again on the big scoreboard at San Antonio basketball games.

Anyway, I was sitting in the audience of "Quick as a Flash," a quiz show hosted by Bud Collier, who later hosted "To Tell the Truth" and other programs on television. The show was done at the NBC studios in Rockefeller Plaza. I had cut work to be in the audience, and when I arrived, they were selecting four panelists — two men and two women — for the program. I had my hand up but wasn't getting recognized. They had two women and a man but needed one more man.

One guy gets called on and says he's Rollo Wainright of Tulsa, Oklahoma. Boring.

The announcer keeps searching, and I'm frantically waving my hand. He stops at another guy, who says he's Emil Willis of Boston. Dull.

Finally, they get to me.

"Zeiger, Larry Zeiger, Brooklyn, New York," I shout, and the place goes crazy. The audience always loved Brooklyn, even though we're about five miles from Brooklyn as we sit in this studio. You would see this pattern on Groucho Marx's "You Bet Your Life" throughout the fifties. Get a guest from Brooklyn, and he had the whole audience with him. Couldn't miss. It was something about the stereotypical Brooklyn character, developed by Gleason on "The Honeymooners," I suppose, or by William Bendix as Chester Riley on "The Life of Riley." A lunch-pail kind of guy who didn't take anyone's guff, who stood up for his beliefs, even if he didn't have a college-bred intelligence. A Brooklyn "guy" was a first-generation American, proud and honest, but often a victim of his own lack of sophistication. And Brooklyn sounded funny. It wasn't Palm Springs or Georgetown or Atlanta. We talked funny, but we made sense. And so Brooklyn could bring the house down 'cause you never knew what was coming next.

I was given the green-light position on the stage. First one to hit his light got a shot at the answer. The first question was worth ten dollars, the second fifteen, and so on. The biggie was a hundred bucks. You could only answer once in each round.

First round. Question: Who was Franklin Roosevelt's first vice president? DING. Green light goes on. "Larry Zeiger, Brooklyn, what's your answer?" asked Bud.

"John Nance Garner, Bud," I shouted.

"That's right, Larry, you've got yourself ten dollars!"

Applause, applause for Brooklyn.

This was all right.

The second question was a mystery voice. "He's right here with us today, ladies and gentlemen," said Bud.

"The first one to recognize his voice, hit your button and light your light!" Offstage, we heard a solid British accent. "I had a wonderful time acting in *Captains Courageous*." DING! "Larry, green button, who's our mystery voice?"

"Freddie Bartholomew, Bud," I said. I'd just seen it!

"That's right! Larry Zeiger of Brooklyn, you've got yourself another fifteen dollars!" Freddie comes out and shakes hands with me. Is this the glamour capital of the world or what?

We roll along, I win a little, I lose a little. Now we're up to the $100 question. Bud barely gets it out and the guy next to me, some guy from Buffalo, hits his button and blows the answer. He's out. He can't answer again in this round.

But now, he figures out the answer. And he scribbles down "Leaning Tower of Pisa," and goes "pssst" to me. I look at him and he whispers, "We'll split the money."

So I hit my button, but it's too late. The buzzer sounded and the round was over.

"Larry Zeiger, Brooklyn, New York, what were you going to say?" asked Bud.

"Leaning Tower of Pisa."

"Ohhhh, that would have been right. We're so sorry."

I won fifteen dollars in all, plus every product Bristol Myers made, used to make, or would some day make. Some haul. All in a huge sack, except the money, three crisp five-dollar bills, which I hated to fold, they were so perfect.

But now I panic. Everyone in that studio audience KNEW I had $15 in my pocket, plus all the Bristol Myers stuff. If I just casually walked back through the audience and out to the elevators, I figured I was New York's number-one holdup target for the afternoon. So I hung a quick turn, saw an exit sign, and headed down the stairs. Thirty flights.

My mother had her usual mixed emotions when I got home with my sack of goodies, most of it for her.

"But Larry, weren't you supposed to be at work?"

All the little mom-and-pop stores near The Corner had their own special place in our lives. You knew the stores, you knew where everything was, and you knew the owners. You couldn't for a minute picture them being anywhere else but in their stores. Jon Cypher, the fine actor, grew up on Hawthorne Street, and has wonderful memories of seeded ryes at Louie's Delicatessen on Flatbush Avenue and of sidewalk singers and street vendors selling fish, strawberries, ice, milk, and vegetables.

Dom DeLuise told me recently of Ralph the vegetable man. "He had a horse-drawn wagon," said Dom. "All the fresh vegetables were displayed so as you stood on the sidewalk, you could see them all facing you on an angle, and there was a giant iron bar that Ralph's scale hung from. My mother would hear him shout . . . V E G E T A B L E S . . . and open her window and wave down to him so that he knew she was coming. I would go on a vegetable adventure with my mother.

"It was a hundred feet from my house and being able to see the horse up close and maybe get a chance to pet him really made my day.

"Ralph was around for a long time. I went from being a five-year-old kid who shopped with his mother to being a seventeen-year-old kid who shopped for his mother. In all those years there wasn't one time when I bought potatoes, tomatoes, broccoli, corn, and spinach, that I didn't pet that horse. Ralph lived on our block. When he died, the horse and wagon was gone from my street but not from my heart."

Murray the barber was, it seemed, destined to always be Murray the barber. The thought of him out of his white smock, not holding a comb and scissors, rapidly going snip, snip, snip (even while waiting for his next customer to ascend the palatial barber throne), perhaps just walking down the street in a tie and jacket, was unimaginable. There were no hair dryers, no "styling," just "Next!" . . . "Next!" . . . "Next!"

And you'd look up from your New York *Mirror,* or *Daily News* or *Post,* watch the snip, snip, snip, and know by the stares of everyone else waiting that he meant you. And you'd

A souvenir photo from Coney Island in the summer of 1944; with little brother Marty and Aunt Sylvia. Oh, did I love Coney Island.

Coney Island picture booth. Howard Weiss, Larry, Arnold Perlmutter.

Below: A classic "team photo" of the Warriors, shot in front of the club-room, which was in the basement of Hoo-ha's home. Hoo-ha himself is at the top left, and Ben the Worrier is at the lower left. I had the good sense to wear my Warriors jacket with my name showing, as I struck a classic baseball-card "on-deck" pose. I was self-conscious enough to remove my glasses for the picture. The photo still sits in my Arlington, Virginia, apartment today.

Above: Stoop of the Warriors' clubroom. *Top, left to right,* Larry, Herb Cohen. *Bottom, left to right,* Arnold Perlmutter, Irvin Kaplan, William Perlberg.

Above: Barbara Nadel's celebrated Sweet Sixteen party, scene of some of our worst behavior. Herbie, looking straight forward over the shoulder of the guy in the front with the light suit; Davy Fried immediately to his left; Hoo-ha, dead-center behind the two girls; Larry, with the glasses, just behind him; and Bucko Buckwalter, mouth agape, behind the accordionist.

Below: Coney Island, 1952. *Top row, left to right:* Shelly Weinstein, Willie Pellbey, Howie Weiss, Mal Auche. *Middle row, left to right:* Elly Gerber, Joe Bellan, Larry. *Bottom row, left to right:* Inky Kaplan, Davy Fried, Hoo-ha Horowitz.

The beginning of my career: emcee at a high school New Year's party at the Colonial Mansion.

July 1961, with my mother in Miami.

Lou Gossett, Jr.

oan Rivers.

Buddy Hackett.

Howard Cosell.

Beverly Sills.

Interviewing Peter Max.

William Bennett.

Eli Wallach.

Richard Lewis.

Henny Youngman.

Larry King today.
Our train stop at The Corner.

Coney Island today.
You can go home again.

go and "take a haircut," not "have a haircut," but "take" one. Today, I still "take a haircut."

You never talked to Murray. He was not a chatty barber. So you read. You brought your *Mirror, Daily News,* or *Post* with you. You'd annoy Murray a little bit because your arms would stick out as you held the paper, rather than give him a perfect covering for your body. And you'd get little hair snips on your sleeves.

In the barber shop you were all equal. Adults and kids waited their turn; age had no preferential treatment. If one of the barbers had a moment, he'd sweep the tile floor clean of hairs, mostly black hairs, with a long broom. The red-and-white barber pole would turn hypnotically outside, and you'd stare at it and try to understand its motion. If you'd "wait for Murray" instead of just taking the next guy free, it meant you were a regular, and other patrons looked at you with some respect. The guy in the next chair might have his face wrapped in steaming white towels, preparing for a shave. The little squirt in the cowboy clothing, crying his eyes out, might be getting his first haircut, perched on the booster seat, with his mother holding his hand. Snip, snip, snip, it would go, the sound of the metal flashing quickly, interrupted at times by the razor strap, prepping for a shave. We feared the razor. None of us would ever consider a barber shave. I've still never had one.

Saturday morning was a big haircut day. The barber chairs were great. You felt regal. You can't really find them quite like that anymore, with the pump, pump, pump, to raise your seat. The makeup chair at CNN is like that, and it always makes me think of Murray. And Murray would snip furiously with his scissors whether he was making contact or not. A little snip, some grease to hold it in place, some powder on your neck, and "NEXT!"

You'd hand over fifty cents as the next customer moved into your seat. And you were gone. And Murray might say, "See you next week," which was something they probably taught him in barber college to encourage business. Like the toothpaste ads that make you think you have to cover your brush, every bristle, with the product, even with a little curl at the end of the squeeze. If they could get every American to do that, instead of covering half the bristles, which is all you need, they've doubled their sales. So Murray would say, "See you next week," even if two weeks would do you just fine.

How we wore our hair was more important than Murray's quick snips would indicate. Unfortunately, Murray didn't give much concern to whether our sideburns came out evenly. He'd give each a quick trim and go, "Next," and sometimes I'd be sitting there, refusing to remove the sheet, staring at the mirror over all the bottles of tonic, turning my head first one way and then the other, asking him to even it out. And he'd try, but by the time he was finished, I'd have sideburns halfway up my head, almost a Mohawk Indian cut. But all Murray wanted to do was say, "Next!" I became famous for a time for my uneven and very high sideburns.

The Chinese restaurant was one of the few real restaurants, the kind where you might tip, that we'd ever venture off to with Mom. Nice and hot on a winter's night. The other food emporiums were the Famous Cafeteria and Feder's Feedbox, where Hoo-ha failed his mind-over-matter test.

The Feedbox was painted light-and-dark green and had about ten booths. It was a burger place, and it was where I first sinned over a meal. That was when I tasted my first cheeseburger, which, by being a combination of meat and dairy, violated all Jewish dietary laws I had been raised on.

My mother thought Feder's should not be enticing the youth of Bensonhurst with such a blasphemous concoction, but eventually, we got her to try one, and, like the sin of pork in chow mein, she admitted it was tasty.

The Famous was a dinner place, cafeteria style. You'd get a card, and as you took each item on your tray, someone would punch the amount on your ticket, until the cashier would total it up. This was a brightly lit place where you could get a meat loaf platter or maybe just a late-night cup of coffee. It invited long conversations and good fellowship. The Famous and The Feedbox were very Brooklyn in that dining could not take place there without kibitzing, exchanging tales about the affairs of the week.

Brooklyn's most famous eating spot may well have been DuBrow's Cafe, near Erasmus Hall High. Beverly Sills told me of her fondness for DuBrow's, how she'd go there before school, read the morning papers, share a hot drink with her father, and eat "those delicious almond horns with cream."

Barbra Streisand hung around at DuBrow's a lot. It was there, she told me, that she dreamed of being an actress. "Never a singer," she said. "Always an actress. I first made it as a singer, but that wasn't my goal. Now, I think of myself as an actress first, because that's what I used to dream about at DuBrow's."

Barbra was such a Brooklynite that "when I went out to the country, I'd get an asthma attack, exactly the opposite of what was supposed to happen. I still have trouble breathing in the country."

There was a Davega appliance store that had television sets in the window, and you'd watch with fascination whenever you passed it, knowing that maybe, just maybe, you might own one of those things some day. Herbie had one of the first, but not in time for the 1950 World Series, Yankees vs. Phillies. We watched that one through the Davega windows. The last all-white World Series.

We'd girl-watch on the corner, and teach each other the facts of life. Occasionally, we may have even been right about them. The fact that I had no father put me at no disadvantage at all in this educational process. No one learned anything about sex from parents. How we came to be so smart that we could pass it on to the other guys is one of those unexplained phenomenons of my time, but we got by.

Coney Island was the scene of some early sexual awakenings for a lot of people. Even though the bathing suits on the girls were very modest compared to today's standards, they were, nevertheless, interesting and at times enticing.

Robert Merrill used to go to Coney Island with his buddies because "that was where the action was."

He told me once how they would "wear our trunks under our school pants so we could slip them right off and head for the beach after school.

"We'd camp out under the Boardwalk. One guy would have a ukelele, and we'd sing all the pop songs. We'd pick a spot under the Boardwalk where the boards were separated, so you could look up between them and check out all the best-looking girls.

"The Young Communist League girls were our favorites. They may not have been the best looking — they weren't the kind to wear makeup — but they followed the party line: from each according to her abilities, to each according to his needs.

"The portion of the beach below the Boardwalk became our make-out resort."

We'd check out all the cars that passed. We knew cars. '51 DeSoto. '49 Studebaker. '50 Hudson. '48 Nash. '51 Packard. We'd play license-plate poker. The numbers on the next car — my plate — will beat the numbers on the following car — your plate.

Once we thought we saw Sugar Ray Robinson's pink Cadillac go by. It was the talk of the street for days. What would Sugar Ray be doing in Brooklyn? Sugar Ray was bigger than Joe Louis among New York's black community. And one day, on our way to the Apollo Theater for a show, we did see it parked in Harlem.

Ray Robinson once killed a man in the ring. A fighter named Jimmy Doyle. Jimmy was the nephew of the guy who owned the billiards parlor near The Corner. We didn't go there much, but he became a major celebrity in the neighborhood.

George Richland Clothing was right by the steps leading up to the el, at 2183 86th Street. You'd lean on the glass counter and negotiate with George. Not that anything was negotiable, but the counter lent itself to the attempt at "hondling" just as he was about to write up your order.

"George, you're gonna sell me these socks for sixty-nine cents. If I bought a second pair, could I have two for a dollar thirty?"

"Okay."

"Well, then you're telling me that at sixty-five cents a pair, you're still gonna make a profit. You wouldn't sell it at sixty-five cents a pair and lose money! So how about selling me the one pair for sixty-five cents; and we both know you're still making a profit!"

It was Beginning Hondling 101, Brooklyn style.

Getting new clothes wasn't as exciting as a new toy, but

there was something about Richland's that made it a nice experience.

And then there was Sam Maltz, proprietor of Maltz's candy store.

Picture Sam Maltz.

You're right.

He was about five six, built like a snowman, with round, chubby cheeks, a little black mustache, thinning hair, a little on the grouchy side, very aggressive about his business, his wife in the back room keeping the books. He was very Brooklyn; he always thought he needed to keep an eye on us. He thought that we were going to steal something. You could never relax if you owned a store in Brooklyn; you were on guard at all hours, not only for theft, but for minor mischief, and the tension that went with having a youthful clientele. Maltz was not cut out to deal with kids, but his lot in life was to run a Brooklyn candy store, and as they say, he had to play the cards he was dealt.

We may not have loved Maltz, but we loved his specialities: egg creams, jelly rolls, chocolate-covered jellies, Creamsicles, Fudgesicles, ice water with cherry or vanilla syrup, club soda with cherry or vanilla syrup, frozen twists, or the best, halvah! Especially chocolate-covered halvah. And Mello Rolls in a cup with sprinkles. Mello Rolls were sort of ice-cream cones, but they weren't scoops, they were more oval-shaped. And frozen twists! Frozen marshmallows, covered in Fox's U Bet chocolate syrup. Definitely sponsored by the American Dental Association. One bite and you're in heaven, even though you're now running to the dentist to repair a cavity.

I had a way of getting under Maltz's skin. One day it was with the newspapers flying all over the street when I didn't put the crowbar weight back properly on top of them. Another day it might be one of my egg-cream negotiations. I would sit at his counter and order two cents plain. This was essentially seltzer with nothing. Cost: two cents.

I would take a slurp, lean across the counter, and say, "Maltz, do you think you could squirt in just a little syrup here?"

If he wasn't in one of his foul moods, he would grunt and give me a quick flash of chocolate syrup. I'd stir it with my straw, and take another sip.

"Maltz," I'd say, "would you happen to have just a little milk?"

And Sam knew I was creating a chocolate egg cream, the greatest drink every invented, but still not known to the western world outside of New York City. One of the great mysteries of life remains why they are called egg creams, as an egg never is used. They are simply made of chocolate syrup — Fox's U Bet — milk, and seltzer, and the closest thing to describing them would be an ice-cream soda without the ice cream. You had to drink them quickly, or the bubbly part created by stirring would flatten and the concoction would lose its artistic beauty.

Egg creams were seven cents, and Sam would explode, make me finish my seltzer and syrup, and throw me out. But I'd be back again the next day and try again.

One day, someone walked by the candy store and just happened to turn the dial on Maltz's sunflower-seed machine, which was outside the store and required a penny for a handful. This day, without depositing a penny, it released the sunflower seeds.

Within minutes, the word was out throughout the neighborhood. Maltz's sunflower machine was broken. Free sunflower seeds.

Lines formed. We took turns getting free handfuls. And inside, Sam Maltz can't believe his eyes. Right there, in front of his store, is the greatest day of sunflower-seed sales in history. A new record had been set at Maltz's machine. He never saw such crowds. He had visions of grandeur. Perhaps a vacation for his family at Grossinger's.

By the end of the day, the machine must have dispensed $5 worth of sunflower seeds.

A bunch of us were outside at sundown as Maltz came out to empty the machine of his newfound wealth.

Nothing.

Not a penny.

Maltz is furious. He's been had and he knows it, and he's screaming that he's been robbed and he'll get whoever did this to him.

Herbie stepped forward.

"Can you prove this, Maltz, in a court of law? Do you have witnesses?"

The ignominy of this was almost too much for Maltz to bear. It wasn't long after that he sold the store and was never seen again. It was said we had run poor Maltz out of Brooklyn.

And that brought the successor to Maltz to the neighborhood, Moe Weinflash. Moe was an immediate hit, for he had a daughter named Carol with the biggest tits ever sighted in Bensonhurst. This is not to say that he attracted a lot of paying customers, but he did get good crowds in the store whenever Carol was there.

One day about six of us were in there, telling stories, shooting the breeze, checking out Carol, when Moe decides it's time for a new store policy.

"Whaddya gonna order?" he asks.

"Order?"

"Yeah, order. You have to order something or off you go."

Well, faced with this dilemma, I sprang into action. The cheapest thing the six of us could order collectively would be a song on the huge Wurlitzer jukebox. By my reasoning, if one of us paid for a song, but all of us were listening, we could all stay.

I selected Frankie Laine's "Wild Goose" and deposited my coin.

" '. . . my heart goes where the wild goose goes.' "

Song ended. We liked it. I played it again.

Then again.

And again.

We played "Wild Goose," oh, thirty-seven times. Maybe I exaggerate a little. It felt like two hundred. To Moe, it sounded like four hundred. He snapped. I suppose anyone might.

Moe was so angry, he practically leaped over his counter and headed for the jukebox. With strength previously unknown to a candy store owner, he snapped the mighty Wurlitzer from its outlet and pushed the monster machine, Frankie Laine and all, out into the street, cursing and screaming and kicking and shouting as he went.

"You want to know where the wild goose goes?" he ranted. "There's where the wild goose goes!"

One of our first television experiences was at the home of Saul Cutler, the very first guy in the neighborhood to own a TV. This was even before Herbie, whose ten-inch RCA Victor didn't arrive for months. There was going to be a major title fight on the "Gillette Friday Night Fights," the kind of thing you'd pay $40 on pay-per-view to see today. It was the battle of light heavyweight Gus Lesnevich, a champion and a war veteran, and Billy Fox, a terrific, and I believe unbeaten, fighter. Everyone was talking about this bout for weeks.

The night of the big fight, Saul's parents set up bridge chairs throughout the living room to accommodate the big crowd. About twenty-five guys were there. Ben the Worrier and Hoo-ha were among the first to arrive to make sure they had front-row seats. The fight was scheduled for 10:00 P.M., after a bunch of preliminaries. Nobody was more excited about this fight than Hoo-ha.

"This is gonna be a war," he kept saying. "When the fight starts, we all gotta be quiet, unnerstand? We gotta be quiet so we can hear Don Dunphy." He would remind us of this as the evening progressed, each time the room would get a little noisy.

We sat through the prelims and were rather rowdy. Hoo-ha never left his seat. He protected it.

Ten o'clock came and went, and we're nowhere near the fighters entering the ring. Finally, around 10:20, there's a commotion on the screen and we know the fighters are about ready to enter. At this point, Hoo-ha stands up and announces, "I'm going to the bathroom, nobody take my seat!" Poor guy hadn't moved since about 7:30. He figured he still had about five minutes or so.

The fighters headed for the center of the ring for their instructions. The bell sounds and out they come. We forget about Hoo-ha.

In one minute and thirty-two seconds of the first round, Lesnevich stops Fox and the fight's over. There were no replays then, so over is over. There's a quick interview in the ring with Gus, and then people start leaving, thanking Mrs. Cutler on the way out for the potato chips.

Hoo-ha returns and sees the commotion. "All right," he says, "this is it. Be quiet now! This is it!"

Poor Hoo-ha. He missed the whole fight. He couldn't believe it. "Where's everybody going? The fight's gonna start any minute!"

Iris Siegel was the princess of Lafayette High School. Every guy's dream. Every guy's sexual daydreams featured Iris in a starring role.

She was Hollywood-gorgeous. Esquire magazine–gorgeous, the kind of girl Vargas would draw lounging in sleepwear, with long red nails, talking on the telephone. I might need a cold shower after I finish writing this story.

One day Herbie, ever the provocateur, said, "Larry, I'll bet you five dollars that you can't get Iris to walk out of school with you, down these stairs, right in front of everyone."

"You mean just walk down these stairs? I don't have to hold her hand or anything?"

"Right. Five bucks."

These were the kind of things Herbie would do. This one sounded easy. Certainly I had enough charm to get Iris to do that much.

So everyone is waiting outside, and I spot Iris, on her way to cheerleader practice. She's in a hurry. But I stop her and say, "Iris, uh, you got a minute?"

She looked at me blankly.

"Would you walk down these stairs outside with me?"

"I'm sorry, I have no time now. I'm late for cheerleading."

I hadn't a moment to lose. "Iris, listen, Herbie Cohen bet me five dollars that you wouldn't do this. I know that you're a nice girl at heart. This isn't a romantic thing. We don't have to hold hands or anything. This means a lot to me. Just walk out of school with me, please?"

Had I humbled myself sufficiently?

"Look, I have no time for this!"

"Iris, look, I'll give you the five dollars. This will take three minutes. Two, maybe. Pul-eeeze?"

"No!"

And she pointed her pretty little nose into the air and trotted off, that gorgeous behind trailing her inside the bouncy cheerleader skirt.

I had to walk out alone and hand Herbie five dollars in front of everyone. It was the lowest point of my high school life. I'm not sure I've recovered yet.

Thirty years later is a high school reunion. It's 1980, and we're all about forty-eight years old. I'm the emcee. We're in a New York nightclub. I'm pretty well known on Mutual Radio now. I'm standing at the bar, sharing some laughs with old friends, and Iris walks in.

She had married a fellow named Asher Dan and moved to California. He became one of the most successful realtors in southern California. They divorced. She is now single, and as gorgeous as when she was eighteen.

She sees me and walks over to the bar.

She kisses me on the cheek.

"Larry, how are you! I love you, Larry! You're my favorite person on the radio. The whole block knows I love you. I listen to you every night, I don't sleep well. And you know something, Larry?"

She moved real close to me now, looked at me in a very sexy way, and said, "I always had a thing for you, Larry, always loved you."

If, at age eighteen, you would have asked me for my five wishes in life, hearing Iris say these words would have been number one.

And I looked at her and said, "Iris, Iris, Iris. Thirty years ago, Herb Cohen bet me five dollars that I couldn't get you to walk down the steps of Lafayette with me. You wouldn't do it. I begged. I offered you the money. You wouldn't do it. It has left a scar for thirty years, Iris."

She had absolutely no memory of the incident. But she said, "You know what it was, Larry? I must have been so flustered being around you that I didn't know what to do."

Goldsmith Bros. was a department store at 77 Nassau Street, catering to the Wall Street crowd. There was a certain dignity to the establishment, but that didn't keep eleven of us from getting summer jobs there. There was an ad in the newspapers looking for employees for the summer shopping season, and that led to the famous Berserk Employees at Goldsmith Bros. tale, circa 1950.

We were all assigned to different departments, told to dress appropriately and to observe the store's conservative image and treat customers with respect. Dainty little bells would ring from time to time, but otherwise, there was a quiet peacefulness to the store which made it a respite from the hustle and bustle of the stock exchanges.

Shelly Weinstein was in the toy department, Ben the Worrier was in the floor-wax department, Herbie was in ring binders, and I was in notebooks. We earned $32 a week, plus, as an incentive, one-twentieth of one percent of everything we sold, which might come out to $4 a month if we were really good.

Well, we're rolling along, doing just fine, when Herbie reads in the newspaper of a new law in New York State, which states in effect that if you work for nine weeks and lose your job, you are eligible for four weeks of unemployment. But you have to be fired.

Had we continued on our career paths, we would have

all quit to return to school. No unemployment. Herbie quickly calculates the advantage of being fired and the date on which to be fired so that it would simply coincide with our plan to quit and go back to school. The way he had it down, we would be drawing unemployment checks for the first four weeks of school.

If this was the pilot for "*I Love Lucy,*" it would not have been bought by CBS. Too unbelievable. But each of us planned our strategy, which led to all eleven of us getting fired on the same day, a day which will forever live in the annals of Goldsmith Bros. history.

Herbie, in the decorum of the ring binder department, began by suddenly recalling his days as barker outside the Rivoli theater. "Folks, step right up here and get your ring binders. The best ring binders in town. Get 'em while they're hot, they won't last long at these prices. Ring binders, all-new-model ring binders, step right up, step right up."

The manager hustled over.

"What are you doing?" he demanded.

"I'm inspired," said Herbie. "I believe in these ring binders. Wall Street NEEDS these ring binders. I can't help myself. I believe that this is the way to move this item. RING BINDERS! GET YOUR RING BINDERS!"

I was in notebooks. All sizes, all shapes. They were stacked high on a wall, and a ladder on wheels was required to reach the high shelves. The main rule of our department was, never roll the ladder until checking to see if anyone was on it. My boss, Mr. Steel, was on the ladder. I gave it a roll which might have qualified me for the '52 summer Olympic ladder-rolling team. Steel hit the side wall hard and nearly fell to his death. I may have overdone it a little.

Ben the Worrier triple-waxed his floor to demonstrate the wonders of new Beacon wax for his customers. They had to close the department for safety reasons when it became too slippery for passage.

Shelly Weinstein started up every wind-up toy in the toy department, which pretty much captured the frenzy of the day. In the end, all eleven of us were fired, and we all went across the street to Chockfull o' Nuts to celebrate our four weeks of unemployment.

I came close to not graduating from high school. My future was definitely in the balance. You needed a 65 average, and it was going to be a close call. My mother, anticipating the possibility of this great humiliation to her son, the son who had skipped second grade, went to school and begged the principal to let me graduate. She invoked the name of Eddie Zeiger, who had died and left her Label fatherless, making it necessary for him to sometimes help out at home and fall behind in his schoolwork. Of course, Eddie had been dead almost seven years, and I had never lifted a finger to help, but as they say, it played well in Peoria. Mom could get theatrical when she had to.

As it happened, it wasn't necessary. I got a 66 and breezed in. The previous class having forever spoiled graduation ceremonies at the classy Brooklyn Academy of Music by wrecking the place, we held our ceremonies in the crowded Lafayette gymnasium. I was pleased that they called us up in alphabetical order and not by class rankings, but in either case, it was a long wait.

SIX

DAHJUHS

IN MY NEIGHBORHOOD, if you said a guy was hitting .287 and it turned out he was hitting .283, your credibility was shot for a year. Minimum. It would be a long time before you would even dare to offer up another fact. No point to it.

We took our baseball very seriously. The Dodgers defined our borough. They were lunch-bucket guys who lived in the neighborhood and played ball in heavy flannel uniforms for a living. If they played well, we loved them. If they didn't, we called them bums and let them hear it. We'd run 'em outta town. They knew where they stood because we were not lacking in any pretension at all. And in the little field they called home — Ebbets Field — they heard everything we said.

My father was a Yankee fan. That he was a baseball fan at all was surprising, for he was an immigrant, and most fans discover baseball in their youth and grow with it. It was unusual for an adult to become a new fan, but my father was an exception. He first settled in Manhattan, and perhaps that is why he rooted for the Yankees, who appealed more to the New York crowd. You wouldn't wear jeans to Yankee Stadium. You couldn't get a box seat; they all went to the Wall Street people. They were easy to hate and had a very WASP-ish image, although many of the names who defined the Yankees were ethnic — Babe Ruth, Lou Gehrig, and Colonel Ruppert were all German, Phil Rizzuto and Joe DiMaggio were Italian, Lefty Gomez was a Spaniard, and Joe McCarthy was Irish. Maybe it was Edward Grant Barrow, the general manager, or Charles "Red" Ruffing, or Bill Dickey, who created the WASP image. There was something about the way they all carried themselves.

DiMaggio was the one Yankee we couldn't hate. He had too much grace and style for that. He was just too damn good. If he wasn't the best player of all time, he was certainly the best of his time. Dodger fans could appreciate talent, and DiMaggio somehow stood above our hatred for the Yankees.

I came to know Joe in later years. He served on the Orioles' Board of Directors when Edward Bennett Williams owned the team. I would have liked to have Joe on my program, but he always declined. He knew I took phone calls, and he knew someone might call and ask him about Marilyn Monroe. Joe didn't like surprises, and he didn't like to be embarrassed. So he never came on the air with me. That would be a thrill for me.

A few years ago I saw Joe getting dressed in the locker room before the Cracker Jack Old Timers Baseball Classic in Washington. He was wearing only a T-shirt, about to slip on his jersey, when a TV crew turned and began to tape him.

"Hey," he snapped, "don't shoot me when I'm in a T-shirt."

Shaken, having been scolded by the Yankee Clipper himself, the crew turned away.

Joe simply would not put himself in a position where his dignity might be compromised. That is why he stopped playing in Old Timers games in the 1970s, and why he stopped putting on a uniform in the eighties. If he couldn't hit like Joe DiMaggio, or look like Joe DiMaggio, he didn't want the public to see him.

The Dodgers won pennants in 1916 and 1920. They were the Robins then, managed by Wilbert Robinson, and that's the only reason I can think of for writers still calling them "The Flock" on occasion when I was growing up.

After 1920, things went bad in Brooklyn, and they didn't win another pennant until 1941. I was eight then, and I don't remember much about that season, although I had probably just begun to become a fan and listen to older kids talking about them. The '41 Dodgers had Dolph Camilli, Billy Herman, Dixie Walker, Cookie Lavagetto, Pete Reiser, Joe Medwick, Mickey Owen, Kirby Higbe, Whitlow Wyatt, and a twenty-two-year-old shortstop named Pee Wee Reese. They were the forerunners of the players who would become the "Boys of Summer" and Brooklyn fell in love with those guys. Like their successors in the fifties, these players took on an aura that said, "We belong here." We imagined that they spoke in Brooklyn accents. We pictured them leaving Ebbets Field with lunch pails and walking home to their little Brooklyn homes in the neighborhood. They just seemed like our kinda guys.

Red Barber had come over from Cincinnati in 1939 to broadcast the Dodgers on WOR radio. Larry MacPhail, who had run the Reds, now was charged with taking the Dodgers from near-bankruptcy, and one of his first moves was to bring Red with him. Very quickly, listening to the Dodgers on the radio became a way of life in the borough, and Red's voice carried the message. He pronounced it "Dah-juhs" but it sounded so right. Eventually he brought his style to television, WOR Channel 9, where his understated manner blended perfectly with the medium in which the pictures could tell the story.

You could not have selected a more unlikely person to become the heart and soul of the Dodgers and the messenger to the faithful of Brooklyn. Red was a southerner with a pronounced accent. He was also learned and scholarly. He did not fit the growing image of "dem Bums," an image to be cartooned across the *World Telegram* by Willard Mullin and in the *Daily News* by Leo O'Mealia. Red was culture, delivered in an easy style from a baseball diamond. His honesty gave the franchise credibility and force-fed us measured doses of integrity and honor. Whatever Red was selling, we were buying.

He was a broadcaster. It was not beneath him to shill for the sponsor, but he made it fun, and he made it honest. Sometimes today you read about the "growing commercialism" in baseball telecasts. Try this out: when a Dodger used to hit a home run, Red would drawl out that it was an "Ollllld Goldie!" and he would slide a carton of Old Gold cigarettes down from the broadcast booth via the backstop, where the bat boy would catch it and present it to the lucky batter as he crossed home plate. If you think "This Bud's for you" gets in the way, imagine an Old Goldie!

Or you might hear that a special "guest" had come into the booth for a plug. It might be, say, Robin Roberts of the Phillies, and it would go something like this:

RED: Well, Robin, nice seein' ya here.
ROBIN: Well, Red, nice to be here. I'm sure feeling good.

RED: Well, you're sure looking good. Did you shave with
    Gillette this morning?
ROBIN: This morning and every morning, Red. Gillette
    Blue Blades. You get ten for a dollar forty-nine.
RED: Gillette Blue Blades I hear!

Even we knew Robin was reading a script.

As Red was the Dodgers, Mel Allen was the Yankees. We
hated Mel. He always had great players and winning teams
to work with, and since he undoubtedly enjoyed his days at
the ballpark, that gleefulness in his voice after another Yankee win was painful to hear. Mel was from the south, too,
but his accent wasn't as pronounced. The fact that Brooklyn
could embrace Red, who might just as well have come from
Asia as Mississippi, was remarkable.

Red was thirty-one when he came to Brooklyn. Baseball
broadcasting was new to New York, lagging somewhat behind other cities. He brought it all to life in a hurry. Nothing
about his work made us feel we were hearing the infancy of
a new medium.

Barber became the earliest voice in my lifetime, other
than my parents. His voice on the radio was the most important element in my becoming a Dodger fan. I never gave
his accent a second thought. He was my conduit to the
game. To this day, when I hear his voice, I am transformed
back to my fire escape on 83rd Street. Before the days of air
conditioning, the fire escape was our porch, our escape
from the stifling air of the third floor.

Brooklyn had fire escapes up and down almost every
structure. They were red or black, government-issue in appearance, and must have made architects cry. Very ugly, but
required by fire laws in days when every construction material could go up in flame. They were small porches out-

side windows with forty-five-degree ladders to the next landing, until you could reach the ground. We used them to simply climb out the window and get a breeze. They were not comfortable, but they were our penthouse terraces. And in our little world there, the radio could be our companion.

I didn't need a "field of dreams." I could close my eyes and Red had me right there, in Ebbets Field or Crosley Field, or Sportsman's Park, or Braves Field, or Forbes Field, or the Polo Grounds, or Shibe Park, or Wrigley Field. I knew them all, just as I knew all the umpires, all the coaches, and of course, all the players.

Jon Miller, the Orioles' current announcer, gave me a gift not long ago of the radio broadcast of the second game of the 1949 World Series. Brooklyn vs. the Yankees, Red and Mel, together. I played it in my car during a snowstorm in January. Suddenly, it was 1949 again, and the brilliance of Barber was right there.

"Well, Mel," he said, "now yesterday we had these two strong ball clubs go scoreless until the bottom of the ninth. And then Mr. Henrich hit one which barely made it to the seats in this big ballpark. Now today, we have Mr. Roe and Mr. Raschi, and while these are certainly formidable hurlers, one can hardly expect another one–nothing encounter."

And Mel said, "I sure doubt that, Red, we're not going to have another one–nothing game today."

Two and a half hours later, the Dodgers had a one–nothing victory to even the Series. Mr. Roe had beaten Mr. Raschi. And Mr. Barber was brilliant. He gave us a dimension we hadn't heard from other announcers. Others dealt in hyperbole, in plugging the players, the team, the league. Red was laid-back, low-key, and very honest. He was distinguished, the way he used "Mr." so often. And he sounded

like a news reporter, not just an employee of the club selling tickets for the next home stand.

One of the thrills of my career has been getting to know
Red, even working with him. I was on Channel 4 in Miami,
doing a weekend interview segment on a six and eleven
o'clock newscast, which was produced more like a feature
magazine than the hard-hitting weekday newscasts. Prescott
Robinson was the anchor; Red did the sports, and my interview segment, on tape, followed Red's. I'd talk to Jackie
Gleason, or Paul Newman, Arthur Godfrey, Stan Musial; whoever might be in town.

Since it was on tape, I got to watch it. And the best part
of the program would be when Red would say, "Those are
the scores, and now, here's Larry King."

My first line, on tape, would be "Thank you, Red." I tell
you, the first time I watched that at home my heart went
through my head. Later he was a guest on my own radio
show, and not long ago, he asked me to write the introduction to a new edition of his book "The Broadcasters." It was
one of the great thrills of my life.

While I started listening to Red in 1940, I didn't go to my
first game until 1944, after my father had died. My cousin
Bernie took me. He was married to Aunt Bessie's daughter
Irene, and he had spent two years helping out as a bull-pen
catcher for the Yankees. He had been an All-City high school
player, not quite good enough to play pro ball, but good
enough to catch warm-ups in the Yankee Stadium bull pen.
I wish I had the memory of going with my father, but he
worked six days a week at the bar, and I guess he was just
too busy, or thought I was too young.

It was a bright and beautiful July day when Bernie and I
went to Ebbets Field. And I had the same feelings that Billy
Crystal described so well in *City Slickers:* the walk up the

ramps, the slivers of grass visible through the rafters, and the final expanse of beautifully manicured green in the out-field and infield.

I had one visual surprise that day. I had always thought the back of the infield dirt was diamond-shaped, not round. Newsreels or still photos never gave me a true picture. Red had missed this point, somehow. He couldn't cover every-thing, every day. For six months I remember waiting to find out what a "called strike" was as opposed to just a plain "strike." I was too embarrassed to ask, and kept waiting for Red to explain it. Finally one day, he did. Now I was amazed to see the curved line forming the edge of the infield where the outfield began. I had thought it was shaped like the bases, in a diamond.

The dirt was so brown, the grass so green, the Dodger uniforms so white, the Reds uniforms so gray. "Cincinnati" it said on their shirts. To me, Cincinnati was eighty thousand miles away. It was where the Dodgers went when they headed "west" to play the Cubs and the Cards and the Reds.

Bobby Valentine told me recently that the thing he liked about playing for the Dodgers was how white the uniforms were. I knew just what he meant.

Except for the surprise of the infield dirt being curved, the place was just as Red had said it was. The Bulova clock, the Schaefer Beer sign, all just as he described. Ebbets Field was a double-decked park of which you would never accidentally say "stadium." It had an intimacy. It sat only thirty-two thousand, but in an age where fire marshals sometimes turned their backs on such laws, the Dodgers would sometimes sneak over thirty-five thousand in, in-cluding standing-room seats, for games against the Giants. Duke Snider called Ebbets Field "love at first sight," for all the eccentrics who showed up every day, the one with the cowbell, the one with the tin whistle, the ones with the jazz-band ensemble.

The second deck stacked its rows at a rather steep angle, and your knees would tuck into your chest so they could stick as many rows as possible in there. Over the outfield wall was Bedford Avenue, and when a player hit one out there, the roar of the crowd could be heard for blocks, so that even passing by, you'd know a Dodger had poked one. There were peanut shells on the floors, and they sold beer in bottles, until good sense told them to have the vendors pour them into cups and retain the bottles. Dodger fans could be rowdy, capable of throwing things on the field. One day a fan ran out and beat up the home plate umpire in full view of everyone.

We sat in the first-base stands that day. The bases were so white. The Dodgers won, 4–3. I can still feel that day. The Reds had a left fielder who was, we were told, deaf. "I got it" from the center fielder would have been inadequate. This being a war year, anything was possible. The Browns had a one-armed outfielder named Pete Grey.

You could get a bleacher ticket for fifty cents, but you'd try to get general admission for $1.25 so your seat had a back. The subway ride, a nickel, a hot dog and soda, and a scorecard, and you'd had a day of incredible entertainment for about $3. You couldn't see movie stars in person for that, and to us, major league baseball players were every bit the equal of a Hollywood star.

And so Ebbets Field became a very important part of my life. Anytime I could go, I went. We'd take the West End Express, change trains, and get off at Prospect Park. We'd walk down Empire Boulevard, cross over to Bedford Avenue, and head for the cheapest seats. If the Police Athletic League was sponsoring a trip, all the better. A freebie. If not, we'd buy a bleacher seat and have a great time. I was Larry "General Admission" Zeiger.

The fact that Ebbets Field was part of a "neighborhood," Flatbush, made it part of all of our hearts. This was Major League Baseball, big time, and it was happening right there, down this street. Jon Cypher lived six blocks away. He told me he could hear the cheers from his bedroom window and could tell if the Dodgers were winning by crowd noise, without listening to the radio.

On a weekend, or in the summer, we'd gather outside the ballpark hours before game time — missing batting practice was unheard of. Sometimes an usher would come by and rattle the gate, as though testing that they were still locked in place. But we used to think he did it to torment and tease us into thinking they would be opening any moment. And then he'd walk away.

You might only see Carl Furillo make one throw during a game, but you could see that great outfielder's arm uncork a throw a dozen times during batting practice. That's why you arrived early.

A box seat was out of the question, but once in a while you could sneak down there in the eighth inning or so if the place had emptied out and the ushers weren't looking. To see the players that close was amazing. We knew them from afar by their gaits and their builds, but up close, it was better than seeing a movie star live on the Broadway stage. I took Toby Goodheart to a game when I was seventeen. I went to the Dodger ticket office at 215 Montague Street to purchase box seats at $2.50 a pop. This would be the only time I ever went near Borough Hall. We sat way down the line in left field, but we were in the first row! Toby wore the white cotton dress. I wore slacks and a shirt with a collar, from George Richland's. I tipped the usher a dollar, unheard of in those days. They never even bothered to wipe off your seat in the grandstand. They knew there were no tips to be found there.

Joe Bellam's father, a dentist, or rather, a guy who manufactured dentures, bought the all-night-game-season-ticket plan one year. In those days the Dodgers played seven home games, one against each opponent. The games were special occasions in the borough, especially since the very first one ever played, back in '38, had been Johnny VanderMeer's second consecutive no-hitter.

Joe's father had four tickets to each of the games, and Joe could take two friends. So occasionally, I would be the fortunate recipient and get to see night baseball!

This was an occasion. While you would ordinarily "dress down" to go to the ball game — dungarees and T-shirts — for a night game you would dress up.

When I used to visit with Earl Weaver on the Orioles bench in Memorial Stadium, and the lights would go on as batting practice neared its end, my mind would always go back to those magical nights of night baseball at Ebbets Field. The first one I ever saw was the Dodgers against the Giants. You can only imagine the buildup. The lights were the talk of the neighborhood, not the game, which was unusual. "You mean," we'd say, "you look in the sky and it's black, but you look on the field and it's like daytime?" The answer, of course, was yes, and it remains a wondrous sight today.

When the Dodgers played the Giants, I started hating the Giants early in the morning. By game time, I was out of control. A loss to the Giants would be such a humiliation that I could barely leave home the next day. The only saving grace was that we were almost all Dodger fans. We could commiserate together.

One exception was my own brother, Marty. Somehow, he had become a Cardinal fan. There was some sort of street game he had played in where each kid was a different major league team. He was the Cardinals. He asked me if they were good, and I said they were. He's still a Cardinal fan to this day.

Marty was something. One day we're sitting together and we notice Cookie Lavagetto methodically removing something from his pocket, then putting it back in. Could have been binoculars. The ritual was repeated with enough regularity that we decided Cookie was stealing signs from the Cardinals. I loved it. Marty was appalled.

He found out that the Cards stayed at the St. George Hotel in Brooklyn Heights, the "hotel with the world's largest natural saltwater pool." Eddie Stanky was the manager. So Marty called Stanky and left a message. At midnight Stanky returned the call. Marty never lost his poise; goaded on by me, he identified himself as a Cardinal fan who had seen Lavagetto stealing signs. Stanky thanked him and hung up. Every Cardinal win over the Dodgers after that night we attributed to my brother Marty.

Buying Dodger tickets in advance by visiting the Montague Street ticket window was usually an adventure. I still don't know why it had to be. Sure, Giant tickets were tough, and if the Cardinals were hot and Stan the Man was coming to town, you could see where it could be a problem. But to my memory, every time we went to the ticket window, we had trouble.

There may have been different people there over the years, but to me they were always sixty-four-year-old guys named Shaughnessey. And he'd say through the bars, "Whaddya want, kid?"

And we'd say something innocent, like "Third-base side for Cincinnati, good ticket please."

"You crazy?" He'd make me feel like crawling into the concrete.

"I can give you upper deck, last three rows. Best I can do."

This would be for a Wednesday afternoon with the Reds.

"How about the third-base side for the Cubs next Thursday?" I'd counter. We liked to be able to look into the Dodger dugout.

"What section?"

"Uh, section eight or ten?"

"No good, kid, I can give you upper deck, section thirty-six, partially obstructed. You got a pole there. Take it or leave it."

One day Herbie and I went to Yankee Stadium for a Police Athletic League–sponsored clinic, which featured Billy Pierce of the White Sox. We sat in the outfield as Pierce, a damn good pitcher of the fifties, taught us his craft.

"This," he says, holding up a baseball, "is how you hold a curveball."

"Wrong!" shouts Herbie.

"Excuse me?" says Pierce.

"You hold a curveball with the seams, not across them," said Herbie. It wasn't a question. It wasn't even the question-and-answer period.

And Pierce said, "Well, the kid's got a point. I throw mine a little differently."

Was there a more unlikely messenger than Red Barber, with his southern accent, to bring us the news about Jackie Robinson? But yet, he was perfect. He always gave you the facts. He let you know you were in on history.

We never had any problem with Jackie Robinson. He was

accepted from the getgo because he could play baseball. Those on the Dodgers who couldn't deal with it were traded away. Those of us on the streets thought it was great. We had no prejudice. I'm not saying Brooklyn didn't harbor any prejudices; it did then, it does today. But Jackie's being on the team was never a problem for us. Because, as Red would tell us, "Mr. Robinson is a Player."

I was at the first game that Robinson played in Ebbets Field. It was an exhibition just before opening day in April, 1947. The Dodgers and Yankees, or the Giants and Yankees, used to play a few preseason games for the Mayor's Trophy when they arrived from Florida. Then, on Monday, the Reds would open in the National League, the Senators in the American League. And on this Monday, the Dodgers played an exhibition against their top farm club, the Montreal Royals. Jackie wore a Royal uniform, as he had the year before when he was both MVP and Rookie of the Year in the International League. He played second base that day.

The next day, Jackie was promoted to the majors and broke baseball's color line by starting at first for Brooklyn. He wore a white sweatshirt under his white uniform as though to emphasize the contrast with his black arms. We knew it was a historic moment because all the newspapers told us so, as did Red. But to us, we were more concerned with how he was going to hit. The Dodgers hadn't won a pennant in six years.

Aaron Sobel and I kept a scrapbook of the 1947 season. It was an amazing year, for Leo Durocher had been suspended, and the Dodger manager was the taciturn Burt Shotten, who didn't even wear a uniform. What a contrast from my hero, number 2, Leo the Lip. What a year for baseball in New York. The Dodgers, with Robinson, were winning in the National League, while the Giants, out of the race, were belting 221 home runs for a new major league record.

In the American League, DiMaggio was winning another MVP award, and the Yankees were winning another pennant. And Red was feeding us all the information, including comprehensive summaries of all the other games.

Sometimes Red didn't travel, but recreated the games via the Western Union ticker. Ronald Reagan loved to tell the story about his days at WHO radio in Iowa handling the same task. His punch line was that when the ticker would break down, he'd have the batter fouling off pitch after pitch until the ticker was restored. Red didn't do that. When the ticker went down, he'd tell you it went down, and then fill the airtime with wonderful baseball stories. There was no phony crowd noise, no crack of the bat, just Red and the mike, and the sound of tick, tick, tick, tick in the background.

Jackie played the game so daringly. We never appreciated his talents and his contribution to the game enough. The stolen base was not as fashionable then as it is today; his highest season total was only thirty-seven. But today he'd be a hundred-a-year man. And he did things on the bases which you don't see anymore.

He'd single to right and take a huge turn around first, freezing in his tracks and daring the right fielder to do something about it. If the guy threw to second, we'd all yell, "Chicken!" at the poor sap. If he threw to first, Jackie would race to second — and make it. He had a nervy attitude on the bases that could anger opponents — and win games. Lou Brock told me the game was different now in that players would not embarrass each other with such things. You play hard, you throw at a guy, but you don't embarrass him. They're all in the union together, after all. I don't think that Jackie would have made a good adjustment to that style.

Enos Slaughter was a great Cardinal outfielder when Jackie broke in. I spoke to him once about Jackie's style. He said, "Robinson was playing first base in St. Louis one day. I was running up the line, I stepped on his foot, and I drew blood. He was all right. He just looked at me. I looked back at him. He never said a word.

"Two years later, in Ebbets Field, I doubled off the right-field wall. Jackie was playing second. I gave it one of my slide-in-stand-up slides, and Jackie tagged me right in the mouth. Two teeth came out. And he winked at me. And I said to myself, 'Now that's my kind of man.' This fellow — he remembered."

The integration of the Chase Hotel in St. Louis by the Dodgers was dutifully reported by Red Barber during a broadcast.

Previously, the black Dodgers — Robinson, Roy Campanella, Joe Black, and Don Newcombe — had stayed at a black hotel. This time, according to Red, "A historic moment took place at the Chase Hotel here in St. Louis. Mr. Robinson told Mr. Campanella that the Brooklyn Dodgers stay at the Chase — all of them. To which Mr. Campanella replied, 'No, it's okay.'

"But Mr. Robinson insisted that the Dodgers stay at the Chase. And upon arriving, they all walked into the lobby, where their keys were waiting for them. Mr. Harold Parrott, the traveling secretary, was thinking, 'What am I going to do?' The assistant manager looked up and calmly announced, 'We don't take Negroes.' At which point Mr. Reese, the captain, said, 'The Brooklyn Dodgers stay at the Chase. These gentlemen play with the Brooklyn Dodgers.' And he gave them rooms." St. Louis had been integrated.

I asked Pee Wee about this incident years later, and about the time in Chicago when he put his arm around Jackie in

front of jeering fans. Their relationship was special, especially with Pee Wee coming from Kentucky. But Pee Wee
would only say he did it because "he was my teammate."
What a simple, eloquent statement.

After Jackie passed his early turn-the-other-cheek tests,
he could be himself, which meant a fiery, win-at-all-costs
competitor. Durocher later told me that he was one of the
worst, most profane bench jockeys in the game. When Leo
moved over to the Giants, Robinson would be all over him
about his actress/wife Laraine Day, making suggestive state-
ments about her only to get Durocher riled.

In his later years, when I got to interview him, he was still
the activist, fighting the battles, as he would be doing today.
He didn't want promises — he wanted things taken care of
right now.

My brother Marty had a job on Lexington Avenue across
the street from Chockfull o' Nuts, where Jackie worked as an
executive. He saw him near the end, crossing the street,
nearly blind. It took Jackie more than the cycle of a full
green light to get across, but he walked unassisted, alone in
this little mission, as he was when he first joined the Dodgers and took on bigger missions. I interviewed him six
weeks before diabetes took his life. He was nearly blind,
except for light, but if he felt death was imminent, he never
let on, other than to concede that his prognosis wasn't very
good. He spoke with optimism, with pride, and with anger
over blacks being excluded from managing jobs. He was
dignity and anger all in one, and you had to admire him.

I'd pretend to be Red Barber when I sat in Ebbets Field. I
really wanted to grow up to take Red's job, but, of course, I
assumed he would be there forever. I'd roll up my ten-cent
scorecard — I always bought a scorecard — and pretend it

was a microphone. I'd use Red's expressions — "sittin' in the catbird seat," "tearin' up the pea patch," "bases FOB" (Full of Bums, or Brooklyns), "rhubarb," and especially, "friends." I loved when he called his listeners friends.

Later on, when I wanted to be Arthur Godfrey, I got some good advice from Godfrey himself. "Don't be me," he said, "be you. Then you'll be Larry King and you'll be much more successful."

Anyway, when it was time for Barber to break in a successor, I was only seventeen and not ready. He selected a young redhead from Fordham University, Vin Scully. He brought him along slowly, an inning a day. Vin was about twenty-two. Red called him "The Fordham Flash," the same nickname Frankie Frisch had.

Scully, of course, succeeded Barber brilliantly when Red left for the Yankees in 1954. He's still the Voice of the Dodgers after all these years. People bring portable radios with them to Dodger Stadium in Los Angeles so they can hear Scully tell them what they're seeing.

I wasn't much for autographs or souvenirs, but sometimes we would see a player outside the park. I remember following Dixie Walker to his car. I remember walking alongside Pee Wee for three or four blocks, asking him about his bunting style. He told me he learned it from a guy in high school. I asked him if he was really a marbles champion, and he told me he sure was, back in Louisville, where he used a pee wee instead of an immie, hence his nickname. I was always inquisitive, always asking questions, just like today.

One of the most interesting political figures of the 1980s was William Bennett, who grew up in Flatbush but moved to Washington when he was in high school. Bill went on to become Secretary of Education and the nation's chief drug czar.

"I thought the world was eighty percent Jewish," he told me. "In Flatbush, I had to walk past four temples on my way to Sunday School."

Bill and his brother Bob were big Dodger fans. On weekends they attended games, but on weekdays, school let out too late. So they would go to Ebbets Field and wait by the players' entrance, armed with self-addressed postcards. As the players left, they would hand them the cards and hope they would sign them and mail them autographs. They usually did. Pee Wee Reese even complimented them on a "very inventive idea."

Bill says his brother still has the cards.

While we weren't memorabilia collectors (sorry to say, what with the value of Brooklyn Dodger stuff today), we never lacked for imagination in personalizing the players. We'd play initial games, like, "SS" — Sibby Sisti, "RN" — Ron Northey, "WW" — Wes Westrum, or an easy one like "SM" — Stan Musial. Or we'd play an early form of Rotisserie League Baseball. We'd take three players, and the object was they had to get six hits among them. You'd get 3–1 odds and bet thirty cents to win ninety. As we did this in school before summer vacation, you had to go with the hot springs hitters if you knew what you were doing. Musial wasn't always a good April hitter. Frankie Gustine of the Pirates was, but you had to know your stuff to pick a guy like him.

Comparing players was always an important source of arguments, and I had my one and only fight with Herbie in forty-seven years over just such a matter.

Herbie was the only Yankee fan among the Warriors. He was a big Joe Page fan. Page was the Yankees' ace reliever before relief pitchers became big, and Herbie would walk like Page, carry his jacket over his left shoulder like Page, and hurdle fences like Page would hurdle the bull pen. How this could be, and we would still be friends, is hard to explain. But one day we were going over the starting line-ups for the Yankees and Dodgers, comparing the teams position by position.

At catcher, you could have quite a debate between Berra and Campanella. I guess there was no clear winner there. They both won three MVP Awards and went to the Hall of Fame, so we were smart if we called it even.

At first base, I argued for Gil Hodges, he argued for Joe Collins. I guess the edge went to Gil.

When we got to second, I considered it a lock for Jackie. Hardly worth pausing at second. That's when trouble hit. Herbie actually thought Snuffy Stirnweiss had the edge. Well, not only was Stirnweiss on the downslide of his career, Jerry Coleman had replaced him as the regular. Still, said Herbie, "Day in and day out, you've got to give the edge to Stirn-weiss."

It was more than a sane fan could handle. I lost it. I grabbed for his throat, and we rolled down the street. I banged his head into the curb, he threw me into the lamp-post. In forty-seven years, we haven't even had an argument, save for that one rhubarb.

As I said, Durocher was my hero until he switched allegiances and moved over to manage the Giants. This was an unforgivable act of treason. We hated him from Day One for that.

It's quite hard to put into words the enormity of his action in making that defection. I can't think of anything in sports to approach it since he did that. You would have to think of something like Yasser Arafat renouncing the PLO and running for the Knesset in Israel to draw a parallel which might be understood today. Dodgers just didn't voluntarily become Giants. Jackie Robinson retired rather than accept a trade to the Polo Grounds.

But when he was with the Dodgers, Leo was the club's personality. Billy Martin was much more like Leo than he was like Stengel, whom he always claimed to emulate. Everyone in Brooklyn, even Aunt Bessie, knew Lippy Durocher. He fought with umpires and represented the little guy getting his say. And Leo had style. In the year he was suspended, we saw him often photographed in street clothes, dapper and ready to do the town.

Leo died at eighty-seven, while this book was in production, in Palm Springs, California, and I suspect near the end he was sitting there at his pool, perfectly color-coordinated. How they keep him out of the Hall of Fame is a mystery to me, unless there are still troubled thoughts over his 1947 suspension for keeping company with "undesirables."

I had a brief encounter with Leo when I was working in Miami and he had returned to the Dodgers as third-base coach under Walt Alston. It had to be awkward for both Alston and Durocher. Leo wore his familiar number two, and Alston had his familiar one-year contract.

The Dodgers were coming to Miami to play the Orioles in an exhibition game. I found out the number at Dodgertown in Vero Beach and called Leo to see if I could interview him the next day. He wasn't in; I left a message.

Later, I found that he'd returned the call and I'd missed it. So I tried again and missed again. Again, he returned the call and missed me. We played about four rounds of telephone tag.

So I take my big reel-to-reel tape recorder to Miami Stadium the next day and decide to go after him cold. Out by the batting cage, I approached him, extended a hand, and said, "Leo? Larry King."

He almost exploded. Nothing amusing about it. "You son of a bitch," he roared. "You wasted so much of my time yesterday on the goddamn telephone. You're one royal pain in the ass!"

I'd gotten Leo at his worst. But I got my interview.

When Leo left to manage the Giants, my favorite Dodger became Billy Cox, the classy third baseman from Pittsburgh. The fact that we got an enemy in a trade made him all the more heroic. It was like capturing him. Nobody was better than Billy at third. I was fascinated by his every move. I knew how he stood, how he ran, how he kicked the dirt off his spikes with his bat. I wore number three on anything I had that required a number. I watched his interviews on Happy Felton's "Knothole Gang" when we got our first TV.

One of my best moments in baseball came when I was with Casey Stengel in the Mets' dugout at Miami Stadium in the sixties. Brooks Robinson was walking by, and Stengel says, "Hey, number five — you are the second-best third baseman I ever saw."

Brooks took the bait.

"Who's the best?" he asked.

"Number three, Brooklyn," said Casey. "Better arm than you." Brooks smiled.

Casey was right. Cox was a shortstop playing third. He played with a beat-up glove and did things no one else could. He had the arm and the range, and it enabled Reese to shade over towards second, and Robinson to shade over towards first. It made the entire infield better. Sometimes, if Reese was hurt, Cox would play short, and he was great there, too. I would get a kick just watching Cox throwing during batting practice.

There were no Boys of Summer until Roger Kahn invented the term for his 1972 best-selling book. Cox was one of the best interviews. He was tending bar at some American Legion hall in Pennsylvania when Kahn visited, and he made Roger tell all the patrons how good he had been. It made my eyes tear.

We loved the other Boys of Summer. Snider, I have to admit now, was not as good as Mantle or Mays, but he was our hero. Terry Cashman's song, "Willie, Mickey, and the Duke," makes you think they were all equals, but I know better now. Still, he was "The Duke of Flatbush" and as close as we came to a matinee idol. And he could hit home runs out of that little park. He hit forty or more five years in a row.

Carl Erskine, it seems, had the greatest sense of what it was like to be a Brooklyn Dodger. He verbalizes it well now, but he knew it even then. Pee Wee knew, but he doesn't seem to express it quite as well. Hodges remained a Brooklyn resident after the team moved, and commuted to Shea Stadium from his Brooklyn home when he managed the Mets, but he wasn't as good an interview and not as descriptive. Erskine really had a sense of it all.

Pee Wee was the captain, and his friendship and inspiration on the Jackie Robinson matter made him a beloved figure to all of us, who felt part of what it took to make Jackie feel accepted. One particularly moving night for us was a night we celebrated Pee Wee's birthday at Ebbets Field. We were all given matches as we entered the park, and lit them like a giant birthday cake in his honor. I could have cried.

Don Newcombe was never really accepted by us, although I'm hard-pressed to explain why. I remember him throwing a baseball in my direction one day, which was caught by a fellow behind me. He was the ace of the pitching staff and a physically imposing man. I know it's wrong, but when he lost the opener of the '49 Series, 1–0, to the Yankees, we felt he choked. He lost other World Series games, too, that we thought he could have won. He couldn't win the third game of the '51 playoffs, even though his relief pitcher lost it. I know it's unfair, but we just never warmed up to Newk.

Campanella, while not an activist like Robinson, was a leader. He could command a ball game from behind the plate. Yogi didn't have that. Johnny Bench did. Campy pumped you. He was a presence. More than thirty years have passed since his paralyzing auto accident. He has retained his spirit, and that must be the only thing that has pulled him through many tough medical crises over the years. He has an abiding loyalty to the Dodger organization, which has provided for him all these years, and under the circumstances, one can forgive his defense of the move to Los Angeles. But I don't like to hear him say it, because he was one of us, and deep down, I know he knows better.

The visiting players we had little use for. We booed them all, except for "The Man," Stan Musial, who just took apart Dodger pitching. We respected him, as any knowledgeable fan would. There was a day in Ebbets Field when he hit the painted signs in the outfield showing the distance from home plate — a different one each time at bat. You can't see that in a box score. It can only be registered as a memory in our heads.

Stan Musial not only got his nickname, Stan the Man, in Brooklyn, he made it a second home. He told me that to him, Ebbets Field was like playing a home game. He never felt "on the road."

He said, "There was always something strange happening at that park. You could never say there was a 'usual day.' " An example was a day that Johnny Long, a world-class softball pitcher, was hired to pitch to the major leaguers. Down they went, one after another — all the great Cardinal hitters.

"My manager then called me back," recalled Musial. "He said something about it not being worth it; he didn't want to throw my timing off. It was the best news I could have gotten."

We also tolerated Sid Gordon of the Giants because he was from Brooklyn and because he was Jewish. There weren't many Jewish players, although we'd wonder for years whether some, like Herschel Martin or Hal Newhouser or Saul Rogovin or Goody Rosen were. Rosen and Rogovin were. So was Cal Abrams of Brooklyn. We knew as soon as we saw his nose.

Koufax, of course, was our very own Dodger. He was the twenty-fifth man on the team, a young wild left-hander, forced to stay in the majors because of a dumb bonus-baby rule that kept high-bonus rookies from going to the minors. But Sandy was a Dodger, and we felt closer to the team than other guys from Brooklyn because one of us was down there in the dugout, wearing that Rinso-white uniform with the blue trim and 32 on his back.

Sandy, always reserved, did not like to be embarrassed. He'd wave if he heard a familiar voice, but he'd pretend not to hear if it sounded like he'd wind up looking for a hole to crawl into.

Like the day during Passover one year when Herbie, Hooha, and I brought matzo sandwiches with chicken fat down to the Dodger dugout for Sandy. The Dodgers were playing the Yankees in one of those preseason Mayor's Trophy games. He was just saying, "Go away, go away," in total embarrassment. But Russ Meyer took the matzo, had a bite, and passed it around to some other guys. Even Jackie Robinson tasted our matzo and chicken fat sandwiches. They liked it.

But Meyer proceeds to give up about eleven runs in three innings, and Herbie decided he'd been the hero, "poisoning Meyer so the Yanks would win."

Koufax, always the quiet one, was also more religious than we were. He observed the holidays, and would never sneak down to the box seats with us. It would have been a sin.

When I had my radio program, I interviewed him on tape before a World Series game. He told me that if I was going to play it the next night — Rosh Hashanah — I had to tell the audience that he had done the interview the day before.

The blackest day for us, of course, was October 3, 1951. The 1950 season had ended on a sad note, with the Phillies edging the Dodgers on a tenth-inning home run by Dick Sisler in the last game of the season, at Ebbets Field. I remember Red Barber describing the mixed emotion felt by Dick's father, George, the Hall of Fame first baseman, who was at that time a top scout for the Dodgers. Red told us he was sitting with Mr. Rickey that day. And he watched his son's homer finish off Brooklyn.

The '51 season had begun on a much higher note, and the Dodgers led most of the way, as expected. But in midsummer, Charlie Dressen, the manager, told the writers after a three-game sweep, "The Giants is dead." The quote gave us cause to celebrate.

On August 11, the lead was thirteen and a half games.

Then the Giants began to move. They won sixteen in a row, thirteen of them on the road. Three were against the Dodgers. And the Giants just kept coming, led by Monte Irvin and their rookie center fielder, Willie Mays. What made it worse, this was Durocher leading the charge.

The Dodgers didn't really blow the '51 pennant. The Giants just wouldn't lose. They won thirty-seven of their last forty-four. The Dodgers would go out and take two of three, then the Giants would move in and take three of three. We were all feeling the pressure of one of the great pennant races in history. I was eighteen. This was still better than girls.

We wound up tied for first. Only a miracle saw to it that we held on that long. The Giants had beaten Boston on the final day, 3–2, to hold on to first place. The Dodgers faced the Phillies again and fell behind, 6–1, with the Giants game already complete.

The Dodgers tied the game and sent it into extra innings. In the twelfth, Robinson made an incredible diving catch behind second to nail a liner by Eddie Waitkus. (Take that, Herbie!) A hit would have cost them the game.

In the fourteenth, Robby tagged one off Robin Roberts for a 9–8 victory, forcing a best-of-three playoff.

The teams split the first two games and the third was in the Polo Grounds.

I was working at Associated Merchandise as a mailboy, in Manhattan. We listened to Red on the radio. It was a very special broadcast, because Red knew his audience was composed entirely of Dodger fans. The Giant fans were listening to Russ Hodges on what would become his most memorable broadcast. Since it was a Giants' home game, Hodges's call was also the one picked up by the Armed Services Radio

Network and by a national radio network. So Barber knew his audience was very loyal and very local.

I think you know the story. The Dodgers had a 4–1 lead going to the last of the ninth. Rube Walker was catching; Campanella was hurt. Newcombe was pitching. He got into trouble and Dressen brought in Ralph Branca to face Bobby Thomson, despite the fact that Thomson had homered off Branca in game one.

Thomson hit the "shot heard 'round the world" to complete the "miracle at Coogan's Bluff," the section of Manhattan where the Polo Grounds was located. You have heard, no doubt, Hodges's broadcast many times: "The Giants win the pennant, the Giants win the pennant, the Giants win the pennant, the Giants win the pennant!"

Red Barber was brilliant that day. He gave us the call, and we shared the heartbreak with him. But Red had come prepared. He was always prepared, always had a plan. He passed that trait on to Scully. He knew his audience, and he knew the hurt we would feel should the Dodgers lose. And so he told us about the casualties in Korea the previous year. And he told us, "This ain't gonna be easy." He told us immediately that forever after, "the names of Mr. Branca and Mr. Thomson will be interlocked." And he told us, "We're gonna see the sun tomorrow, friends. And there's going to be a 1952 and other seasons thereafter."

The words helped, but not very much. I took the subway home, feeling as sad as I had felt since my father died. And I came down the steel steps of the Bay Parkway station in Bensonhurst only to find Davy Fried, the one and only Giants fan in the neighborhood, waiting for me on the corner, at the base of the steps. Unless it was Durocher himself, there was no one I wanted to see less at that moment than

Davy Fried. I was crying. Davy teased me. It hurt so badly. And to this day I can see Davy Fried standing there at the bottom of the steps, waiting to let me have it.

The World Series was a blur. Yankees vs. Giants. My two most hated teams. It couldn't be over fast enough.

Four years later, after nearly fifteen years as a Dodger fan, we finally won a world championship. The Yankees had beaten the Dodgers in 1941, 1947, 1949, 1952, and 1953. This time the World Series went to seven games, with game seven in Yankee Stadium. We were prepared for the worst, but Johnny Podres was pitching, and somehow he didn't carry the past with him like Newk and Oisk and Black and Roe and the others did.

And Podres shut down the Yankees, 2–0. With two out Elston Howard grounded to Pee Wee. He threw to Gil and the Dodgers were the world champions! The borough of Brooklyn, my home, was champion of the world. We didn't even represent a city, like every other team. We were just a county, for godsakes. And we were the champs.

I was a grown man of twenty-two when it happened, working at the offices of Silver Shield ("We consolidate your debts"), and the victory came just around quitting time. I heard it on the radio, and still picture Reese's throw to first to end the game. It wasn't quite V-E Day in the streets of Brooklyn, but horns were honking, people were hugging strangers, and everyone was madly in love with our Bums. I was like a kid that day. It sort of climaxed my years of unbridled loyalty. I had lived to see the payback for all the tears I'd shed and all the prayers I'd said. No more "Wait 'til next year!" The only bad thing I remember about that day was that Herbie, the Yankee fan, was in Germany with the

Army. I lost the opportunity to let him have it after all those years that the Yankees had won.

I was already in Miami when the Dodgers made the rumors official by announcing that they would be leaving for Los Angeles for the 1958 season. It was so painful, even from twelve hundred miles away. They said that Ebbets Field had no parking and that the place was falling down. The parking meant nothing to me; we always took public transportation. As for the place being in disrepair, to my memory it was not something we gave any thought to at all, no more so than today's Boston fans think of Fenway Park or today's Chicago fans think of Wrigley Field.

I couldn't continue to root for them. Their 1959 pennant, which included contributions from ex–Brooklyn players Snider, Hodges, Furillo, Gilliam, Labine, Zimmer, Neal, and, of course, Koufax, Drysdale, and Podres, gave me little pleasure. In my heart, I hoped that Duke and Gil and the others were sad, too, for the fans left behind who couldn't share in the victory.

In fact, Brooklyn-born comedian Richard Lewis traces a "lifelong depression" to the Dodgers' departure. He told me that he went to a Mets game in 1963, found Snider and Hodges in Mets uniforms, and "contemplated suicide for the first time."

The lesson, said Lewis, was that "things just get up and leave you. Nothing is forever."

Believe me, I did not sleep better at night knowing that Walter O'Malley, who broke our hearts and abandoned the game's most loyal fans, had gotten a sweetheart deal that no man could refuse. I still hate him.

*   *   *

While baseball was our true love, we were fans of all sports. I was probably more involved as a fan than the other guys, because I'd go to events that the others couldn't care about at all.

We always had general admission tickets to Madison Square Garden, but there were times we stretched them into more. Those were the days of day–night doubleheaders. You would go to see minor league hockey in the afternoon. Then they'd clear out the place and let the new crowd in for the Rangers in the evening.

To beat this system, we would run into the men's rooms and occupy the stalls, raising our legs above the door so that the ushers, checking to make certain the place was empty, would overlook us. We would sit in those stalls for three or four hours until we could hear the fans arriving for the Rangers. Then we'd emerge, disappear into the crowd, and find some place to park ourselves to watch the "Blues."

John Condon was the Voice of the Garden. I always loved New York's public address announcers; they, more than anyone, lent that sophisticated style to New York. Watching the baseball All-Stars get introduced in Toronto recently by the Blue Jays' P.A. announcer was an embarrassment, the way they'd roll out the names of the hometown favorites and try to elicit a greater fan reaction. You couldn't do that to New York fans.

Froggy Winger was our best heckler during hockey games. He could put on this scratchy, froggy voice and bellow at the players. His favorite target was the goalie on the Chicago Black Hawks, a fellow named Al Rollins. Once we happened to wind up right behind him, where two panels of protective glass came together. Froggy decided that this slim opening was the perfect slot for him to get all over the poor goalie.

"You're good, Rollins," he croaked. "You're a good goalie, Rollins," he continued, "but you're a laaaast-place goalie, Rollins, a laaaast-place goalie, do you hear me Rollins?"

Eventually, Rollins had heard enough. With a suddenness so swift that no one could say they even saw it, Rollins skated behind the goal, raised his stick, and managed to hit Froggy in the nose. It was so artful, and none of us had even seen it. But Froggy had a bloody nose to show for his night's heckling.

I enjoyed the Knicks in their early days, and I loved listening to Marty Glickman describe their games on the radio. Basketball was his best sport. He would paint such a vivid picture. I could lie in bed and see the court when Marty was announcing. You knew exactly where everyone was standing, and when the shot was taken, you had a perfect picture in your mind of the movement on the court. Marty invented the word "swish" to describe a ball slipping through the basket without touching the rim, and to this day, I don't know of any word in sports that better illustrates a particular play.

Harry Wismer and Bill Stern gave me football on the radio. They weren't as good as Red Barber, but they were important parts of my youth. We were all Giant fans, but we were intrigued by the Brooklyn Dodgers and New York Yankees football teams, particularly by the odd, two-toned uniform jerseys the Dodgers wore. That rival football league, the All-American Conference, didn't last long, but we were there to lend our support, just as we were there for anything involving a ball or a goal. I saw college football at Yankee Stadium, minor league hockey in Long Island, boxing at Sunnyside Garden, the early Knicks at the 69th Street Armory. If there was a general admission ticket to be sold, I was on line. Or at least I was in a stall in the men's room, waiting for them to blow the opening whistle.

SEVEN

THAT'S ENTERTAINMENT

WHILE WE WERE NOT FAMOUS for being smooth with women, our alter ego was Frank Sinatra. As long as Frank was smooth, we were smooth, for he, more than anyone, set the standards by which we wanted to perceive ourselves.

Frank was from Hoboken, New Jersey, of course, but he so epitomized the spirit of a Brooklyn street guy that we sort of adopted him as being one of us.

Still, none of us really *knew* him. We just knew he was the best thing show business had ever produced. The fact that he worked so hard, and was so available to us only made us admire him more. We would go to the magnificent New York Paramount to see him sing at twenty minutes to nine on a Saturday morning. It cost fifty-five cents, plus you'd see a movie after his show. Not bad. Try that out on Michael Jackson or Madonna sometime.

This great stage would be before us. The band would give you a little overture, and you would see Frank's silhouette behind the curtain. And the curtain would rise and there he would be, in person, bigger than life itself.

We all thought we could sing like Frank, but of course, none of us could, and nobody to this day can. He went through his ups and downs just like we all did. He was good-looking, but he was also short and skinny, and still, he always got the most beautiful girls. Ava Gardner. My god, this skinny guy from Hoboken winds up with Ava Gardner. There was hope for us all. So we envied him and idolized him. He could move fourteen-year-old kids with romantic music. Fourteen-year-old kids today don't know from romantic music.

Frank didn't write his own music, but he interpreted music so well, with such feeling, that he mastered the style of paying tribute to the lyricist simply by interpretation. He could sing a lyric like we wanted to say a lyric to a beautiful girl. When I got to know him, he would explain to me how he would select songs. Barbra Streisand's "People" was covered by many artists. Not Frank.

"What do these lyrics mean?" he asked. " 'People who need people are the luckiest people in the world'? What the hell is that saying? I don't get it. I know people who are really independent; they don't need people. This makes no sense."

He was a perfectionist. You could tell it by the way he delivered a song. Every word counted. His records never sold all that big; he didn't have a million seller until "Strangers in the Night" in the mid-sixties. But he was bigger than records, movies, radio, television. Nobody sold that many records back then. We would go to Sam Goody Records and check out the latest, but our purchases were few.

Joe Raposo, a brilliant songwriter, was doing work with Streisand years later. They were putting together music that related to Brooklyn, for a CBS special. So they drove around Brooklyn, and at one point, near Ebbets Field, someone said, "Didn't there used to be a ballpark here?" Nothing came of it.

Now, it's eight years later, and Raposo is doing an album with Sinatra, and Frank wants two original songs on the album. Out of this comes the idea for "There Used to Be a Ballpark Here." Brilliant. Nothing so captured the feel of Brooklyn, although it could have been about any former ballpark. And Frank threw in a line at the end, "The summer went so quickly this year," and it was a line that just grabbed your heart. Oh, he could put over a song.

When Frank's time to go is upon us, there will be a tremendous loss for those of us who grew up sitting next to the radio listening to him. Tremendous. Those of us who followed him to the Paramount, and then to the movies, and then through the marriages, the Palm Springs years, the retirement, the return. The bad stories never bothered me. He gave us our money's worth and never cheated us.

Anthony Quinn once told me, "Here's a guy you've gone to bed with, woke up with, slept with, romanced girls with. . . . The only thing he has ever done for you is give you a gift, and you didn't even have to buy it."

We had him on "Larry King Live" a few years ago. He had just participated in a tribute to Irving Berlin where he sang "Always." Someone else had performed "Remember." Sinatra was telling me about it and started to demonstrate the lyrics of "Remember" for me. Sinatra was singing to an audience of one — Larry Zeiger — to make his point. He was giving me a private education, and he was performing to me. I got goose bumps.

Here's this kid from Brooklyn who used to sit at eight-thirty on Saturday mornings at the Paramount to watch that stage rise, and Sinatra is singing this song to me.

I'm on national television, but I want to run out and call

everybody I ever knew in Bensonhurst and tell them to turn on the TV, you won't believe what's happening.

I'm humbled by him. We have him on, and you wouldn't think he'd come on and take phone calls, because you'd think he'd feel like people would ask Mafia questions and Kennedy questions and Marilyn Monroe questions and God knows what else. But Frank knows people. He's got the instinct of a streetwise Brooklyn guy. And he knows those people wouldn't call, and they don't.

On all of those subjects, Frank will only say, "I owe the public my best performance, nothing else." Of the supermarket tabloid reporters, he says, "They're parasites and fools. They live off the real or imagined misfortunes of those with infinitely more talent than them." In one sentence, he's cut them down and defined their journalism. Frank knows that if the guy in the street likes you, you're in.

I slow-danced with Toby Goodheart to Sinatra. When I hear Sinatra I think of Toby.

My memories of Sinatra's music take me back to the bedroom I shared with Marty. We had a radio, and Mom had her own radio. Any disputes over what we would listen to in our room were usually settled in favor of me, being the older brother. Marty wasn't old enough to appreciate the romantic feelings Sinatra could stir, but he listened.

Like Mrs. Egghouse's legs, which I knew I liked but didn't know why, those voices in the radio turned me on. From an early age I knew I wanted to be in that box, just like them, making people laugh or learn or just plain feel good. From the days I rolled up comic books and "announced" into an imaginary mike, I knew I could make an audience listen, and I knew I could get gratification from the process. If I could become Red Barber some day, I would be the happiest person on earth.

The radio brought us the Dodgers, but also the news. The immediacy of it was wonderful. The stuff I would read in the papers the next day was already known by the radio announcers. They were transmitting news to me within hours, or even minutes of its occurrence. I work at CNN now; they do it twenty-four hours a day, and I still marvel at it. How could we improve on this in the next century?

It is said today that the competition for the entertainment dollar is tougher because there are more options. I disagree. We lived in an age before television, and we still had a full menu of distractions from schoolwork and family responsibilities.

Sinatra at the Paramount was only one example. On a big date, you might go there. But we saw stage shows at the Strand or the Roxy. You could see Bob Hope. Bing Crosby. It would cost five cents to take the West End Express into Manhattan, and we had no problem with riding the subways late at night.

There was a thriving immigrant theater in Brooklyn, where Europeans could be entertained as though they were home. Vincent Gardenia made his acting debut at a place called the Fifth Avenue Theater in Brooklyn. They did shows for the Italian community there. He tells a story of moving an audience — as I did at my bar mitzvah — when he was a teenager, doing a play called *Il Zappatore* about a peasant farm family, sacrificing to send their son to Rome to study law. When he graduates, he is embarrassed about his family's humble ways, and he lies to his girlfriend about his heritage. The family overhears the lie and throws him out of the house.

Soon afterwards, the mother becomes gravely ill, and the father goes to Rome and meets with his son at a grand ball. The farmer tells his son about his mother's illness, and the son returns home to make his peace. It was an emotionally charged audience of immigrants that saw Vincent perform that play. When the lights went on and they went out into the streets of Brooklyn, so far from Rome, many would be wiping tears from their eyes.

For an ordinary date, we would go to local movie theaters. We had the Brooklyn Paramount and the Brooklyn Fox. There was a restaurant in Brooklyn called Junior's. It was a date place. It was our answer to Lindy's, which was the big place to go in the city.

Did I wish I had more money to spend? I hardly gave it a thought. It wasn't a high priority. I wasn't bombarded by things I coveted and couldn't afford. We didn't see "ordinary" families on television sitcoms owning more than we owned. We had our Police Athletic League tickets to sporting events, and you could see live shows and movies for fifty-five cents. You could see a Broadway matinee for $1.80. It's hard to believe as I write this, but I remember that. I had afterschool jobs and could make enough to earn those small but memorable treats.

We had Prospect Park and Coney Island and Luna Park, museums and Ebbets Field and Madison Square Garden.

And we had the J.

The J was located at 7802 Bay Parkway; it was a focal point for us, a gathering place for social and athletic activity, a magnet for the entire region within Brooklyn which we populated. The Warriors were only one of the clubs in the JCH. There, we came into contact with many other people, like Koufax, Elliot Gould, or Gary David Goldberg. It was like a "Y", and we would sometimes play against YMCAs in basketball. If you played high school ball, you weren't eligible for a J team, but if you didn't, this was a high level of competition and you played teams from all over the city.

There were activities that went on in the JCH which were intended for parents. Our relationship to the J was fairly well restricted to the athletics. There were rooms I never knew existed at the J. I knew the locker room and the gym.

We had terrific sports leagues at the J. The stereotype of Jewish kids not being good athletes died in this place. Koufax was our best example, but not the only one. The competition was at a very high level.

These youth organizations were a great magnet for the kids of Brooklyn. If you weren't into sports, there were other activities. Many tried theater in such settings for the first time.

Eli Wallach of Flatbush joined a Boys Club and had his first taste of drama there.

"It was here," he related, "that I was first taken with the thrill of the stage. I could get up in front of people and mimic the different mannerisms of the characters I portrayed."

Dom DeLuise found inspiration for performance arts all around him in Brooklyn. He told me, "There were many things that worked for you as a performer; the fact that your father was an Italian immigrant, and your mother spent most of her time cooking, and your brother was a used-car salesman, or your sister was trying to raise three kids. They help make you funnier.

"You could refer to them when you went to confession on Saturday, holy communion on Sunday, and had enough sins to go to confession on Saturday, again.

"You could talk about going to church and getting the

giggles and having the nuns walk down the aisle and giving you a shot in the back of the head that would bring tears to your eyes.

"But the thing that made an audience cheer and applaud and root you on was when you mentioned you were from Brooklyn. It was like you got a hole in one."

Sports competition spilled out into the streets when things weren't always as organized as they were at the J. We had Association Football and two-hand touch, where the quarterback was everything. There was four-corner slap ball, stickball, kick the can, hit the penny, marbles, stoopball, flipping baseball cards, ring-a-lievo, three feet off the ice, Chinese handball, and punchball. For a good stickball game, we would steal Dora Horowitz's mops, decapitate them, and close off a street for a big game. The cops let us do it, unless someone complained, and then we'd drop the stick into the sewer and hide the evidence.

One day the cops actually lined us all up against a gate by an empty lot on suspicion of stealing a mop handle. We had hidden it. I looked right at the cop and said, "What other evidence ya got?" Tough guy.

A good stickball game could be played with as few as four guys, two on a side, and some young kid, maybe Marty, to do the catching for both sides and maybe get an at bat or two that "didn't count" along the way. If you had six guys, you would play two men behind the pitcher, or maybe a different catcher for each team.

In stickball you had the constant pitcher-batter duel, just like in the big leagues. The batter could imitate the stances of his favorite players, or try and switch-hit. The pitcher felt all-powerful, uncorking the Spaldeen at his top speeds; maybe thinking he was throwing a curve of sorts. Guys would be on the sidelines, leaning on parked cars, their caps pulled down closely over their eyes, intense on the competition. The fielder's attention might wander, and then, all of a sudden, instead of the whoosh of a miss would come the marvelous sound of wood against rubber, as the Spaldeen soared down the street. The rare catch of a fly ball into bare hands was a bonus out, for when it was hit, you expected to reach base safely. Most outs were strikeouts, or grounders back to the pitcher. Every kid who ever played stickball in the streets of Brooklyn can remember the longest shot he ever hit, the moment when it all came together.

In the summers, we would play on into the night. The street lights barely provided enough luminescence, but we didn't care.

How did we decide what to play? It usually depended on how many people showed up. Some things were ritualistic. You played punchball on Sunday mornings, sometimes for a little money.

You learned who your enemies were. If one of our Spaldeens landed in Mr. Saborio's front lawn, he would cut it in half on us.

Spaldeens were little hollow rubber balls, perfectly suited to many games, manufactured by Spalding. We heard that the rubber in the Spaldeens came from the Far East, and sure enough, during the war, the rubber supplies were cut off from Japan, and there was a shortage of Spaldeens. For this alone, which seriously affected our way of life, we hated the Japanese. I think we hated them more than the Germans, for whom our hatred extended to German shepherds, schnauzers, and Dobermans, but the Japanese were directly affecting stickball games in Bensonhurst.

Spalding stopped making Spaldeens in the 1980s. It was a sad day when I read that.

We played a major league level of kick the can. The idea of the game was, well, to kick the can. Everything else you made up as you went along.

Stickball was played in one of two ways, either with pitching it on a bounce, or hitting it without a pitcher, just bouncing it yourself and whipping the thin bat through it.

Punchball was a variation on stickball; all the rules were the same except you used your fist to make contact. Money would be bet on these games, and sometimes, what we considered "big-time" punchball players would come to our neighborhood and all we would do was watch.

We were avid Association Football players, which was basically two-hand touch. This was a game with a quarterback and receivers, and all receivers went long.

One day Herbie threw me a long pass. I fell, and someone fell on me, breaking my right pinky. But I never noticed it or felt it, and I went back to the huddle with the pinky bent strangely to one side.

Herbie called signals. "Okay, Howie, you go out to the sewer; Ben, you cut left at the Studebaker. Four Fingers, you go deep and turn at the Oldsmobile."

I looked down at my hand and almost passed out. That finger is still bent funny today.

By late summer, we would listen to the College All-Stars playing football against the defending NFL champions, and that would signal the beginning of the throw-the-football-around season. We all got inspired by that game.

We'd play roller hockey, and a lot of basketball in the park, at the J, and down by the water. Herbie firmly believes that Koufax developed his arthritis playing basketball with us in Brooklyn, getting knocked into the steel pole that supported the backboard.

In stickball, you were measured by the number of sewers

you could hit the ball, there being a sewer drain on each block. Occasionally, you would run into a three-sewer man.

Marbles were big, and nothing was more precious than your purlie shooter, the special somewhat larger marble you would use to hit and win other marbles. It would be a tough blow to lose your shooter.

Stoopball was made for Bensonhurst, which had America's best stoops. If you caught the ball on a fly, ten points. On a bounce, five points. If it hit the edge of the stoop and flew back at you, a hundred points. First to get a thousand wins. It was said that one day, someone in Bay Ridge did it in his first ten throws, but there were no witnesses. That would, of course, be a record.

The stoop was also a social mecca for us. Before we discovered The Corner, we had the stoop. We'd sit and talk, or play stoopball, or argue about sports or what was on the radio the night before. I learned about broadcasting from having conversations on the stoop. I would account for "dead air" by announcing passing cars or pedestrians. And I would reconstruct movies, ball games, whatever.

Ask Art Modell, the owner of the Cleveland Browns, about his growing-up years in Brooklyn and he'll tell you about the stoop and the stoopball games, and stickball and punchball and Spaldeens and roller hockey with a wooden puck sawed from a log branch. He knows. He was there.

We didn't do drugs, and we didn't drink. Sniffing airplane glue was something we heard about. We did smoke too much, but all we ever heard that it did bad was stunt your growth, and we didn't buy that.

*   *   *

We had parties, sometimes in the Warriors' clubroom, sometimes in the J, sometimes at the school gym, and sometimes just at people's homes. Arnie Perlmutter was always one to just say, "C'mon over; let's have a party."

Davy Fried was going out with a girl named Barbara Nadel. Barbara's parents had money, and they decided to throw her a Sweet Sixteen party.

Now because she was going out with Davy, it seemed appropriate to invite the Warriors. But the thought of twenty of us at the party was too much for her parents to bear. They had this suspicion that we couldn't be trusted to behave.

So it was agreed among them that six of us would be invited as a token of friendship for Davy, and that our six names would be drawn out of a hat.

Davy came to the clubroom and explained the process to us. We have a drawing, and as luck would have it, the six guys most likely to misbehave get picked. Me, Hoo-ha, Herbie, Bucko, and two others.

When Mr. Nadel heard who the six were, he made an immediate decision that we would each sit at separate tables.

This was going to be almost like a wedding, a major catered affair, white linen, the works. There could be no rowdiness, no juvenile behavior. We nodded our understanding.

From the Nadels' standpoint, this was a disaster from the beginning. The fourteen Warriors who were not selected in the draw waited outside the catering hall, and we kept sending food out to them. It was winter, it was cold, and these guys were standing outside in the snow. What could we do in good conscience? We would go onto the buffet line, fill up a plate, and send it out, then get on line again. The food was running out quickly.

Each of the six of us chipped in five dollars to buy Barbara a jewelry box. I was assigned to make the purchase. I didn't do well. She thought it was a scarf box.

Now, enter the entertainment, an accordionist. He entered the room just as we were seated, and Herbie was at the table closest to the door.

"Who's party is this?" he asked.

Herbie pointed to me. "It's that guy's party," he said. "Larry Zeiger."

So the accordionist turns to me and plays, "Happy Birthday, Dear Larry," and Barbara goes into shock.

Now the dancing begins. Barbara's cousin was my date. She was the only one at the table I knew. Herbie's over there, Hoo-ha's over there, Bucko's over there. A big tureen of soup is served. I'm a big shot, I say, "Allow me to serve."

And I spilled hot soup on Barbara's cousin and scalded her on the arm. Blisters, everything. A mess.

At one point, I coughed. Herbie thought this was a signal to start a cough wave, so he coughed, and then Hoo-ha coughed, and then Bucko, and then the other guys.

Bucko fell into the punch bowl during a dance. His face went dead into the center, greasy hair and all.

"Needs more sugar," he announced.

When it came time for Barbara's special spotlight dance, just her and Davy, the sentimental moment of the evening, Hoo-ha wasn't paying attention. So Herbie, picking up on this, walked over to Hoo-ha's table and says, "It's time to dance."

So the bandleader announces, "And now, let's all honor Barbara and her special friend, Davy, with a spotlight dance in honor of her special day," and Hoo-ha and his date are on the dance floor, waltzing away.

What a calamity that party was. You may find this hard to

believe, but Barbara and Davy got married and are still married today.

Oh, but the radio, how I lived for the radio. It swept me away. If there was a secret decoder ring available from Ovaltine so you could better enjoy Captain Midnight, I was the first one at the post office to mail in my application.

"Captain Midnight," or rather, "Ovaltine presents, 'Captainnnnnnnn Midnight'," was on Mutual Monday through Friday at 5:30. Even if it was still sunny out at that hour, I would find a way to listen. I hung on every breath. At the end of each show, you would get a clue. They would give you a number, and you would use your secret decoder ring to translate it to a letter. The code would change. And at the end, after all the figuring out, the message would be something like, "DANGER LURKS!"

Mutual was always the network that would take chances, do things a little differently. You knew by the sound of a program if it was on Mutual. Like Fox today, they were trying to carve their own niche against CBS, NBC, and ABC, and sometimes that niche meant trying programs the big three wouldn't touch. Mutual Broadcasting System began as a group of stations that couldn't compete with the big three, but collectively, they might pool their resources and get some interesting programming. WOR was the New York station, the station my program was first carried on when I later went to work for Mutual.

Mutual had "The Shadow" on Sundays at 5:00 P.M. "Gangbusters" was on Sunday evenings. I enjoyed the programs, but I hated Sunday nights. There was always the impending doom of returning to school the next morning, unprepared. There was always some assignment I hadn't completed, some test standing out there, proving that indeed, danger lurks!

On the other hand, Saturday was the best day of the week and still is. I absolutely love Saturdays. No school, and no school the next day. And as much as I love working today, it still means no work, and no work the next day. It still gives me the same buzz.

So on Sundays, you would listen to Drew Pearson on ABC at 6:00 P.M. and begin to feel serious about the impending week. He gave you political commentary, and he was interesting. He was Jack Anderson's mentor. I was an avid listener to the political commentaries on the radio. Some guys I bought; some guys I hated. But they made me react. Radio was reaching out and grabbing me by the throat and tugging at my emotions. It made me laugh or cry, and I thought the political commentaries were far more educational than the stuff I was learning about in school, which was, of course, delivered without any particular political slant, other than pro-American.

At 7:00 P.M., Jack Benny was on NBC. At 8:30 it was Fred Allen. You would switch the dial to ABC at 9:00 to listen to the latest gossip from Walter Winchell, an incredible radio personality, who became known to a later generation as the narrator on "The Untouchables" on ABC TV. You never said "Walter Winchell." "Winchell" was enough. It seemed like such a perfect name for his hard-driving style. Sometimes when I write my *USA Today* column, I think I'm doing Winchell.

At 10:00, an up-and-coming host named Garry Moore hosted a game show called "Take It or Leave It." I identified this program with the close of the weekend, and the thought of it depressed me. When Garry went into television with his game shows and variety shows, I still associated his voice with the end of the weekend.

Monday afternoons would bring the return of the daily serials. "Superman," 5:15, WOR, each weekday. "The Mutual Broadcast System presents, the 'Adventures of Superman'!" I can still hear the wind as he flew.

The Green Hornet, with his faithful assistant Kato. Kato was Japanese. On December 7, 1941, he became Filipino.

At 5:30, over on ABC, we had "Jack Armstrong, the All-American Boy." Our parents liked for us to listen to this one. He "set a good example."

Edward R. Murrow, still a godlike name among newscasters, delivered the day's events on CBS each weekday at 7:45 P.M. His voice was the voice of authority. No one questioned a report from Murrow.

Monday nights at 8:30, we had the "Arthur Godfrey Talent Scouts" on CBS. What a radio genius Godfrey was. He remains my inspiration on the air. He took chances. He wasn't afraid. Sometimes they worked, and when they didn't, he was still on top.

I remember Godfrey doing a live commercial for peanut butter. This is radio. And in the middle of the commercial, he spreads the peanut butter on a slice of bread and proceeds to eat it.

Now you know how long it takes to swallow peanut butter and begin speaking coherently again. Didn't bother Godfrey. You could hear him savoring the product. He took a chance, and the sponsors trusted him. America trusted him.

Godfrey took a chance on a comic named Lenny Bruce on his "Talent Scouts" program. Bruce did a bit in which he was a guy at an ad agency hired to handle the Hitler account. Hitler jokes weren't funny for a long time after the war, but

Godfrey took a chance on Bruce, and the bit was a riot.

Lenny's bit was a spoof of the ad business as well as of Hitler, because so much of Hitler's success was in his propaganda machine.

"So, what have we got here?" said the agency type. "Guy named Schickelgruber. A painter. Wants to rule the world. Send him in.

"So, Schickelgruber, have a smoke, take a seat. Can we get you anything? What can we do for you?"

"Kill all the Jews."

"Whoa, hold on. This ain't gonna work. You've got to carefully develop a project like this. You can't do a hard sell. You need to create an image behind the campaign. First, I would suggest an easier, friendlier name. Schickelgruber's gotta go. Whaddya think of Hitler?"

And from there, the bit would take off. Lenny could offend a lot of people, but he could use black comedy to score a lot of points.

Godfrey also did a slow-and-easy morning show, which you'd catch if you were home from school with the flu. I told him this the first time I met him. I was working in Miami when he moved down there in the mid-sixties. He had a show there, and I got to know him. I even got to co-host his program with him, and to emcee his birthday party.

"Don MacNeil's Breakfast Club," live from Chicago, was a big morning show. And on WOR, you had "John Gambling," which is still on that station with another John Gambling, a grandson.

Mondays at 9:00, you had the "Lux Radio Theater." This was the type of show with actors reading a script and dropping the pages to the floor. Loved it. I went to see shows like this in person.

Tuesdays at 9:00 was "Amos 'n' Andy," sponsored by Rinso on NBC. You can't imagine how big this show was. When this show went to television, with a black cast, it got a bum rap. It was considered racially offensive and hasn't been rerun on television in a quarter century.

I really don't think it was offensive. There were a few characters that would embarrass any group, but we later had "The Goldbergs" on television, and that was ethnic and had the same lazy characters. Kingfish, on "Amos 'n' Andy," was one sharp guy. He was cool. We loved Kingfish. Some people would yell and scream, but I'd love to see this program back.

"Amos 'n' Andy" gave NBC Tuesday nights. It was the lead-in for ""Fibber McGee and Molly," and Bob Hope, and they both had huge audiences, too.

Bing Crosby was on Wednesday nights at 10:00 on ABC. Nat King Cole was his piano player.

Fridays were big. "Information Please," at 9:30 on Mutual, the best quiz show ever. I learned more from that show than I did in four years of high school.

At 10:00, "Gillette presents, 'The Friday Night Fights.'" Don Dunphy, your announcer. A legend. A great broadcaster. A gentleman in a tough sport, making sense of it all.

Bill Stern did a sports show presented by Colgate late Friday nights on NBC. He had a reputation for stretching the truth, but that seemed to build his audience. There was also the classic Stern story about his doing a football game, having the wrong runner, and then having the guy lateral to the correct runner in time for the touchdown.

Now Stern's assigned to do a horse race. And the line is "Hey, Stern, how ya gonna lateral a horse?"

Bob and Ray were heroes of mine. Two of the greatest

comics show business ever produced. Herbie and I would do their bits on The Corner.

Bob Elliott did this radio announcer, Wally Ballou, and since I was determined to be a radio announcer, I loved Wally and appreciated all the nuances of the character. Most of the time, he would simply greet his audience as ". . . ly Ballou," because either the engineer had forgotten to open his microphone on time, he had jumped his cue, or he didn't talk right into the mike when he was supposed to. In any event, a lot of people never got the ". . . ly Ballou" joke, but since I was now the neighborhood radio "expert," I was able to educate the guys on The Corner.

". . . ly Ballou here, and ladies and gentlemen, we are witnessing the most fantastic halftime show I've ever seen at a college football game. Yes, it's a salute to the American automobile. And you've never seen anything like it. They've got big cars, small cars, pickups, station wagons, trucks, convertibles, two-doors, four-doors, two-tone, whitewalls, antiques, luxury cars, and sedans. It's the most amazing halftime show in history."

At this point Ray Goulding would interrupt Wally and say, "Wally, you're facing the parking lot."

And Ballou would casually adjust his tone and say, "Ah, sorry about that ladies and gentlemen, I was positioned in the incorrect location."

I went to see Bob and Ray do their radio show. The day I went, Wally Ballou was interviewing the president of a company that built fire engines.

"How many of these babies do you sell a year?" he asked.

"Oh, we sell one every two or three years. They don't put on a lot of mileage. If you buy one it lasts a long time, and most fire departments have one by now."

And Wally would ask things like, "What happens if the fellow on the back of the hook and ladder turns left while the driver up front is turning right?"

Anyway, while the interview is going on, the factory catches fire. The place is soon engulfed in flames. But as Wally starts to panic, Ray Goulding's character just goes on with the interview, acknowledging, "We just build 'em, pal, we don't know how to put fires out."

Finally someone calls the fire department. But, wouldn't you know it, this was the one town where they'd never sold a fire truck. The place burns down. Great stuff.

Bob and Ray took us to pogo stick conventions, and to gatherings of the STOA, the Slow   Talkers   of America.   The   national   headquarters was   in   Glens   Falls,   New   York. And all the time that Bob Elliott is getting this out, Ray Goulding is growing increasingly, and riotously, impatient, until the audience is just as agitated, but howling with laughter. There may never have been two voices better skilled at radio. A lot of people remember them for their Piels Beer ads as Bert and Harry Piels, the Piels Brothers. That was a terrific advertising campaign.

Just as no one would go to the movies on Monday nights when "Amos 'n' Andy" was on radio, the advent of television created the same situation on Tuesdays for Milton Berle. Trust me, there has never been a television phenomenon like Uncle Miltie — not "I Love Lucy," "Gunsmoke," "The Beverly Hillbillies," "All in the Family," "Dallas," "Cosby," none of the top-rated shows. Milton Berle, if they had ratings then, had to have a one hundred share of the audience. What was the point of investing in a television set if you didn't watch Berle?

Since Herbie's family had a set, a little ten-inch RCA, we would gather at his apartment on Tuesday nights. We would watch John Cameron Swayze deliver the news at 7:45, and then Berle would go on at 8:00, with the singing Men from Texaco in their gasoline-station uniforms introducing the program. I suppose recalling his gags now, the bits in drag, the slapstick, might not seem funny to later generations. But we howled. The whole family howled. It was a shared family time, sitting on the plastic-covered furniture, eating candies out of cut-glass serving pieces. Berle put television on the map and made it a family event.

A couple of years ago, I was the subject of a Friar's Club roast in California. Berle was the emcee. Everyone was funny; it was a great event. I couldn't help but sit there and marvel that this kid from Brooklyn, who used to sit in front of Herbie's ten-inch TV set enthralled by Uncle Miltie, was now being roasted by him at a dinner in my honor. And the material was not the stuff that the family could watch together.

To meet all of these people as my radio show took hold was a thrill beyond belief. Red Skelton. And Jackie Gleason, "The Great One," who made us laugh and cry with his range of characters when he started on the Dumont network, Channel 5 in New York. Gleason became a South Florida resident, and I got to know him very well.

In fact, I knew Gleason as early as 1964, and wound up emceeing his annual birthday bashes for years. He was still on top then, starring in movies, hosting a weekly variety show, and selling millions of albums of romantic music. I was a kid who used to stare at him on Herbie's set, watching Joe the Bartender and the Poor Soul and Reggie Van Gleason and, of course, Ralph Kramden of Bensonhurst on "The Honeymooners." Now he was a frequent guest on my programs in Miami, and I was the host of his birthday parties. Gleason and I "bonded" almost from the time I first met him because of the Brooklyn connection. Two guys from Manhattan would not have the same shared experiences. Ours were not urban experiences so much as neighborhood experiences. When Gleason knew you were from Brooklyn, he wanted to know what street, what candy store, what subway station. His life in Brooklyn was rougher; his father had split, there was more sadness to his childhood. But he knew about friends and he knew about the ties that bind, and it was easy to be Jackie's friend if you had that Brooklyn connection.

I was such a big Gleason fan as a kid that I would faithfully watch his summer replacement show, which he had little to do with, apart from helping to select guests. It was as though, in his honor, I wouldn't abandon the time period CBS gave him. Tommy and Jimmy Dorsey hosted the summer show, and that was the first time I ever saw Elvis Presley. He sang "Blue Suede Shoes." His torso was all in motion; he was not shot from the waist up like they did on the Sullivan show later. But I didn't think I was watching a phenomenon, or a "phenom," as they're called in baseball. I remember thinking, "What the hell is this?" Rock 'n' roll was a coming crusade, but the Warriors were just a little too old to embrace it. We were caught in the crosscurrents of a changing culture. We liked Sinatra, Bing Crosby, even Johnny Ray. But the coming of Elvis was just a few years after the age where we might have been sucked up by the magic he obviously had.

Gleason, much older than we were, spotted it. He was a genius. Gleason was no fan of rock 'n' roll, as his sappy romantic albums would attest, and by his later, very public, denunciation of some more daring acts, like The Doors. But

Jackie booked the acts that went on his summer replacement show. And someone told him that there was this hot kid from Tupelo, Mississippi, named Elvis Presley, who had a hit record.

Gleason was a quick study. He didn't need two minutes with Presley. One minute. He sized him up as an honest kid and decided he'd put him on. He always knew what he was doing.

He even tried to give Elvis advice that makes sense to me. "Don't do room service, kid," he told him. "No matter how big you get, don't ever set yourself up so that you're trapped and can't live a fairly normal life. Touch the people. Stay one of them. Don't get lost, Elvis."

It didn't work out that way for Elvis, of course. Gleason knew what he was talking about.

The legitimate theater was affordable to us. No, we couldn't go once a month, but you could save up a little and get to Broadway. I took Toby to see Phil Silvers in *Top Banana,* which was the first musical I ever saw. Sometimes, we would slip over to New Jersey to the notorious Hudson Theater, which was a burlesque house. They had comics and strippers. You didn't really go to see the comics, but they were always funny, so you didn't mind them at all. We would take the West End Express into the city, then a bus to Jersey. It was a long trip, but the excitement of going to this forbidden place as a pack was worth the effort. We saw Gypsy Rose Lee and Lily St. Cyr there, the two most famous strippers in the world. Compared to a typical sitcom on TV today, you barely saw anything. But to wide-eyed kids from Bensonhurst, this was erotica as it was meant to be, teasing, forbidden, fantasy-filled. You'd dream about this stuff for months, in anticipation.

Nightclubs have a special memory for me, too. This was the heyday of New York's nightclubs — the Latin Quarter, the Copa — and while they were a little pricey and out of our league, the aura of their presence loomed over the Manhattan nightlife scene. It was like the Statue of Liberty and the Empire State Building; you never actually *went* there, but it was a feeling of power in being a New Yorker that they were there.

Don Rickles was from Brooklyn and still tells me that the biggest thing in his career was his success at the Elegante Nightclub, on Avenue J in Brooklyn. The owner was a fellow named Joe Scandore, who became Rickles's manager for more than thirty years. The Elegante was a stepping-stone to the Copa in those days. It was everything a Manhattan nightclub was supposed to be: dark lights, little round cocktail tables, a tuxedo-clad emcee making the introduction, a small combo behind him, with the drummer getting your attention with a little roll-and-cymbal clash. Smoke would fill the room, and nobody would say, "Thank you for not smoking." There were girls in brief outfits selling tobacco products off trays, and you could tip the maitre d' for a better table. You'd order Manhattans or highballs or the ever-popular dry martinis, and the spotlight would go to the stage and you'd catch the show.

Harry Morton was a fabled talent agent and nightclub owner from Brooklyn, who at one point ran the Elegante. Harry had a thing about shined shoes. To him, they were the measure of a man.

Problem was, Harry couldn't get a quality shine in Brooklyn, at least not to his satisfaction. But he had a chef at the Elegante, a black man who had the best shine Harry had ever seen.

"Where do you get that shine?" asked Harry.

"Place up in Harlem, where I live," said the chef.

That was all Harry had to hear. Every two weeks, he would give his chef a dozen pairs of shoes in a sack to bring to Harlem for servicing.

After a couple of years, his chef quit. Harry was in trouble; how was he going to get the shoes shined?

Before departing, his chef gave him the address. So Harry gathers up his twelve pairs of shoes and treks up to Harlem on his mission.

He walked into the shoe-shine parlor, and three narcotics agents pin him to a wall, accusing him of dealing drugs.

Harry was screaming, but the narcs proceeded to rip open all of his shoes in search of the booty. He showed them his driver's license when they asked for identification, but when they saw "Brooklyn," they were convinced he was a dealer. Why would a guy from Brooklyn be getting his shoes shined in Harlem? In the end, the City of New York paid for his shoes.

Brooklyn was by no means a wasteland for these clubs. Buddy Hackett of Williamsburg remembers the newspapers listing as many as thirty in Brooklyn.

"These were the places guys like me played after the war," he says. "On nights I played, the guys in the neighborhood would all come and watch my routine. Their support kept me working, because if a comic could draw people into a club, he'd be asked back. The encouragement I got from my friends and the number of clubs available in Brooklyn were very important. You could work every weekend and really polish your skills."

For summer entertainment, the Catskills were the place to be. The Jewish Alps. Every hotel had a lineup of stars, no charge for the show, just there to add class to the place and pack in the tourists. Buddy Hackett practically "owned" the Concord. Berle played the Catskills. Sid Caesar played the Catskills. Red Buttons was gigantic there. Eddie Fisher; every Jewish mother's dream. Morey Amsterdam, Eddie Cantor, Georgie Jessel, Sam Levenson, Robert Merrill, and Jerry Lewis, who became identified with Brown's.

I worked one summer as a busboy at Grossinger's, the most celebrated of the Catskill resorts. You would take a Short Line bus there, up Route 17 before the New York State Thruway was constructed. It was about a seven-hour trip from Brooklyn. You'd stop at the Red Apple Rest in Tuxedo, N.Y., for a burger, and then on to the mountains, the bus driver grinding his gears as he negotiated the famous Wurtsboro hills.

I got laid that year on home plate at the Grossinger's softball field. She was a married woman who had come up for the summer. Her husband only came up on weekends. I was the busboy at their table. We took a walk one evening, and, well, talk about scoring. Right on home plate. I was a guest speaker a few years ago at the New York State Broadcasters Association convention at Grossinger's and told that story, right with Governor Mario Cuomo in the room. It was hard to resist.

I was with this woman on a Thursday, and now it's Saturday morning, and, bingo, her husband's sitting next to her at the table that I'm bussing. I was so nervous I spilled butter all over her and knocked into her husband. He asked me why I was shaky, but after lunch the next day, he gave me a big tip for the week.

I doubt if any other region in America has a Catskills to complement its metropolitan area. Maybe in the world. Here you'd escape from the dirt and foul air of the city, take this long drive upstate, and suddenly, in the middle of nowhere, would be these enormous resorts — palaces — filled to the brim with your own people, all these other Brooklyn types who had made the seven-hour trek up the Wurtsboro hills for the privilege of getting away from it all for a few days.

The Catskills were dotted with bungalow colonies and with elegant hotels, elegant at least in a setting where you were as likely to pass outhouses and stray chickens as you were unlikely to pass a seafood restaurant.

Those few families who actually lived year-round in Sullivan County, New York, lived in near poverty, far from civilization, and one wondered how they ever found their way there. We knew of tales of mountain people, who could spook you if you ran out of gas and had to get out of your car.

But suddenly, you would turn into this driveway, all but hidden by huge trees until you were right upon it, and there you would be, stacked on line, waiting to check into these solid and stately mansionlike main buildings at the resorts.

You might time your arrival for dinnertime, but by the time you parked the car, stood on line to register, got to your room, unpacked, and made your way to the dining room, you had blown your dinner. What a mistake.

Meals were what the Catskill resorts were all about. Into the dining halls would troop a couple of thousand of people, right on schedule; 7:00 A.M. for breakfast, noon for lunch, 6:00 P.M. for dinner. So anxious would they be that they would start to line up forty-five minutes early, even though the seats were assigned, and no one ever ran out of food. At dinner, women wore cocktail dresses and mink stoles with handbags and dangling earrings and white gloves. Men wore jackets and ties despite this being a vacation. It was the code. People had no problem with the rules of the house.

The waiters and the busboys lived for tips and we were characters unto ourselves, each with some act, each seemingly becoming familiar with the guests, even though the tables recycled into new people every few days. The better our personality, the better the tips. We were the focal point at mealtime, with people seated at round tables for eight, seated with strangers, sharing the roll baskets, the water pitchers, the relish trays, the butter, the cream cheese spreads.

The menus listed a dozen main courses, and if you didn't like one, the waiter would bring another. Everything was included in your stay. The waiters knew they could befriend you by making this amazing offer: "Try the pot roast; if you don't like it, I'll bring the chicken." Imagine trying this at the Palm.

No matter how full you were, you never skipped a meal, for there was this feeling that you were "paying for it," and it would be a sin to let the food go to waste. So just a few hours after some enormous breakfast of pancakes and rolls and French toast and bagels, you would haul yourself back to the dining room, with no appetite left, but, hey, it was lunchtime.

The hotel lobbies never seemed to change much. If pinewood walls were there in 1947, so were they there in 1956. If Art Deco, with endless mirrors, marked your journey through the lobby and to the grand staircase, there they were ten years later.

The day's activities, always optional but always neatly outlined on sign boards or handouts, included all the popular pastimes of the day: card games, softball, horseshoes, Ping-Pong, rowing, mah-jongg, basketball, biking, hiking, the ever-popular Simon Sez, and, of course, swimming.

There were indoor pools and outdoor pools, and at each would be acres of lounges, occupied by white bodies male and female, fat and slender, muscular and frail, bald and bushy. They would all be greased with Coppertone, with sunglasses or hats for extra protection. Men smoked foul cigars and sometimes wandered over not in bathing trunks but in baggy shorts with knee-high socks, sandals, and those ribbed, sleeveless, unflattering undershirts. This was not a pretty sight.

The lounge acts after dinner drew the big stars, who enjoyed trying out material on tough crowds (translated: the shows were free so people didn't always pay attention), and who enjoyed coming up for a free weekend at a resort. The non-Jewish acts must have felt as though they were working a foreign country, particularly at mealtimes, with the heavy fare of Eastern European Jewish delicacies like blintzes, borscht, herring, lox, and matzo-ball soup. You couldn't smoke from Friday night to Saturday night — *Shabbes* — you couldn't eat dairy with meat (so, no butter for your rolls on a meat night, no cream for the coffee), and Friday night you'd play the audience after they'd come out of religious services.

Sam Levenson was one of the greatest comics of this era, and one of the top draws in the Catskills. The Jewish crowd was perfect for his kind of show. And yet, it was always hard to think of Sam as a comic or a showman, for he was a former schoolteacher, whose easy nature and brilliant observations on life itself were hilarious as well as wise. (Myron Cohen was another great talent in this genre.)

Sam would walk on the stage and talk about things that touched everyone in the audience. If he had an older crowd, he'd do a grandparent shtik.

Sam worked in the tail end of an era when comics were not political or sexual. Their routines tended to mirror everyday life. And they found in the Catskills an audience that didn't care so much about getting away from it all as they did about laughing about it all.

Not until the 1970s did the crowd gentrify, and by the 1980s, kosher food was no longer standard. But in the heydays of the resorts, the postwar years into the sixties, the Catskills were meant to make Jews comfortable.

Among the regulars at the hotels would be the social director and his staff, the maitre d', the lifeguards, the bellmen, the proprietors of the small shops off the lobby, and even the owners, who were treated like celebrities.

The best known was Jennie Grossinger, whose family owned the best resort of them all, Grossinger's. This was the standard for all the others — the Concord, the Nevele, Kutsher's, the Pines, Brown's, the Brickman, the Fallsview, the Flagler, the Raleigh, the Tamarack Lodge. Jennie was more than an owner; she was a hostess who treated her guests like family, and that little touch gave her a great reputation and made for endless repeat customers. The hotels were open year-round, and had plenty of winter sports activities, but the drive was tough in the winter, frightening even, and the business relied on their summer seasons.

"This is my nineteenth year up here," you'd hear someone say. "We honeymooned here in forty-eight; these are our children," someone else might mention. When guests got comfortable, they liked to return; they liked to feel as though they had the run of the place, knew their way around; were remembered and respected. Jennie knew how to create that feeling.

Those of us who worked at Grossinger's lived in the bunkhouses, about ten to a room, about a half mile from the main house. Some grumbled about the conditions, but we got the same food as the guests, which was terrific, and we could sneak in to see the shows, and I got to watch a lot of great basketball action. The hotels would have teams, made up of staffers, and they would play other hotels in hot competition. One year Milton Kutsher signed up Wilt Chamberlain as a bellhop so he could play for the Kutsher's team. For black kids up from the cities for a Catskill summer, it marked their first great adventure in American cholesterol heaven.

The shows were wonderful, in glitzy nightclubs with long tables where you would run a tab and see, "live, on stage," Eddie Cantor and Sammy Davis, Jr., and Sinatra, and Sid Ceasar and Berle and Martin and Lewis, Bojangles, Red Buttons, Buddy Hackett, Liberace, Robert Merrill, Georgie Jessel, and Red Skelton. The social director, who earlier ran the Simon Sez competition on the lawn, was now in a dinner jacket as emcee for the evening, and, "Hey, I know that guy," was the feeling you'd have when the spotlight would hit him in center stage. Oh, what a time that was.

One day when I was bussing at Grossinger's, a pal and I somehow got a lift from Buddy Hackett, who was headlining at the Concord. All of a sudden the three of us came upon some Catskill mountain man who was shooting birds. Buddy was outraged; Brooklyn guys didn't know from shooting birds.

He stopped the car and got out to argue with the man. It was a gutsy thing to do, as the guy had a gun and all. But Buddy was persuasive, talking about orphaned newborn birds, the cruelty of the sport, and so on. He almost had the guy in tears. Finally, the guy walks off, puts his gun in his car, and drives off.

At that point, Buddy opens his truck, pulls out a shotgun, and announces, "Now this is my territory!"

Buddy had this famous bit in which he played a Chinese waiter, and while he could have picked that up from any of the hundreds of Chinese restaurants in Brooklyn, he may also have researched it while out with his friend Jan Murray one day in Brooklyn.

Jan, a tall man with excellent posture, bent over one day and couldn't get up. His back had gone out and he was in terrible pain.

Buddy had a chiropractor he wanted to get Jan to, but Jan was in such agony, he couldn't even get into his car. So Buddy had to put him on the hood — like a dead deer — and slowly drive him to this guy, a Chinese chiropractor with one arm. No kidding. And sure enough, the chiropractor gave Jan one chop to the back, and Jan has stood straight to this day.

Just as riding the subways on into the late hours didn't frighten any of us, neither did a visit to Harlem. We had absolutely no fear of it. We would go to the Apollo Theater to catch the acts and never gave a thought to violence.

We took a 2:00 A.M. subway home and never looked over our shoulders or experienced fear. It was a great time to be a New Yorker and savor all the city offered.

We called black people Negroes. Never niggers. Not ever. Sometimes someone might say "colored," and our parents used a Yiddish word, *Shvartzer,* which had a derogatory sound, whatever it translated to. I didn't like that word then, or now, and am always uncomfortable when someone pulls that one out of a hat.

Herbie took a trip to Florida once and came back full of stories about separate water fountains, bathrooms, and Negroes sitting in the backs of buses. We had an awareness of this from reading the *Daily Worker* and other leftist material, but to hear Herbie describe it made it much more dramatic, and made us all quick to anger. And the first thing I saw when I got off the bus in Miami in 1957 was a water fountain that said "COLORED."

A cousin of mine married a black guy, which was rather

unheard of at the time. I was in Miami. My mother, being a product of her generation, was in physical pain over this. I suspect she would have been a more enlightened woman on the subject today.

I was the one who broke the news to her.

She looked at me and said, "Has she lost her mind? Has she totally lost her mind?"

The fact that I was pretty calm about this news made her feel I, too, had gone crazy.

But it really wasn't a big deal to me.

It was when I was in Miami that the liberal influences on our lives took hold. In Brooklyn, we were all talk. There didn't seem to be much opportunity to demonstrate any action.

In 1962, I had Malcolm X on the radio with me. Until that time, our black heroes were athletes and musicians, guys like Jackie Robinson, Louis Armstrong, Sugar Ray Robinson, Nat King Cole, and Jesse Owens. Malcolm X sort of opened my thinking. Why weren't we aware of black businessmen? Black anything other than athletes and performers? Why didn't we ever see them in commercials? I had never even thought of that. And so his presence on my program ended my period of blind isolation. It was no longer possible for me to be a "liberal" just because I liked watching Robinson play baseball or Duke Ellington play piano. We could no longer be afraid of blacks who had political and social thoughts. They were as entitled to their views as we were. And if there were to be social changes coming, they would have to come from political thinkers, not from athletes and musicians.

Malcolm X was not a beloved figure in the white community. There was something frightening about him. But he made me think, as he made thousands of black people think. And I started to change and get more involved. I became interested in the civil rights movement in Miami.

In 1966, Martin Luther King, Jr., tried to check into a motel in Tallahassee, Florida. The reservation was made under Reverend King. The clerk accepted the reservation.

My lawyer, Toby Simon, was also working with Dr. King. He called me up and said, "Larry, Martin Luther King is going to check into a motel in Tallahassee today, and I don't think they're gonna let him in.

"I think he's going to sit down on the porch, and I suspect they'll arrest him for trespassing. And we're prepared for this, and we want to use this as a way to test the trespassing law."

The Civil Rights Act had been passed by Congress and signed by President Johnson, but sure enough, here was a little forty-unit mom-and-pop motel off the beaten track. We all knew that the Act protected people at big places. But this was a little family-run hole-in-the-wall.

"Would you like to come up for this?" said Toby. Would I ever! This was an opportunity to witness a little bit of American history.

Toby was prepared to walk in the front door with Dr. King, as his lawyer. I was invited to accompany them.

The three of us walked through the screen door and up to the desk. There was a mob behind us, complete with police cars, reporters, black and white onlookers.

Dr. King said, "I have a reservation."

The clerk checks his records, looks up, and says, "We don't take niggers."

I couldn't believe it. I could believe this could happen, but I couldn't believe this ignorant son of a bitch would make this statement in front of Martin Luther King, trailed by his lawyer, journalists, and a mob in front.

So Dr. King turns, exits the screen door, and sits down on the porch. I'm there, too, along with Toby.

We make small talk for a while.

"My real name is King," he said to me. "Is yours?"

"No." I smiled. "It's Zeiger. Larry Zeiger. The owner of my radio station changed it when I got down here from Brooklyn."

He laughed. It was the only laugh he had that day.

The owner of the motel came out. He was not a real redneck in the mean sense, just a slow-talking good ol' southern guy with a potbelly, suspenders over his undershirt, and a cigar.

"What is it that you want?" he asked Dr. King.

And I was right there when Martin Luther King, Jr., looked up at him and said, "I want my dignity."

I got a chill. It went right through me. Up my bones to the back of my neck.

"I want my dignity." He spoke it so well. And he was absolutely right. It was outrageous that he couldn't stay at that motel. I may have realized this in an abstract sense until that day, with my sheltered Brooklyn liberalism. I'd never been to the front lines. The indignity of this moment was never fully captured for me by the *New York Times* or even by the *Daily Worker*. And I felt his silent rage.

They arrested him. He did not look like a person of dignity as they took him away. But eventually, that motel and every public accommodation was included in the Civil Rights Act. The dignity followed. This was just another step for Dr. King. It was an awakening for me.

*   *   *

The telephone was a source of entertainment as well as communication for us. It was as though it had just been invented, like the ballpoint pen. When the ballpoint pen came out, Herbie studied it and said, "How can we use this to our advantage?"

As for the phone, it was nothing like today. The thought of calling Herbie, who lived only two blocks away, would have been unthinkable.

"You're *calling* Herbie?" my mother would say. "Two blocks away and you're calling him on the telephone?" But we must have done it enough; I remember his number: BEnsonhurst 6-8274. I was BE 6-2724. Mine was a party line; you'd share the number with another household. You might pick up the heavy black phone and hear talking, so you'd hang up, because if you didn't, they knew you were listening in, and they knew who you were.

The phones had straight wire with fabric around them; no coiled extension wire. We never imagined that the rotary dial would one day be obsolete, but we're almost at that point today. Plastics, lighted dials, colors, different shapes, cordless, cellular, owning your own, were all unconsidered. We thought the existing boxy telephones were so miraculous, improving on them was unnecessary.

I had a good telephone voice, and we made a lot of calls from Maltz's. I even called Arnie Perlmutter's girlfriend for him; he thought I was smooth on the phone.

If we were at Maltz's and we had a coin, it got used. If not in the juke box, it went into the coin phone. We might call a religious broadcast, sort of a forerunner of Dial-A-Prayer, and say, "This is the Lord. Any messages for me?"

Or we might call Guy Lombardo's agent. Lombardo was a New York institution playing New Year's Eve at the Waldorf

Astoria. His rendition of "Auld Lang Syne" simply *was* New Year's Eve. He was a recording artist and his band played many concerts, but he found this niche as Mr. New Year's Eve and built his reputation around it.

So we'd call Lombardo's agent and ask if Guy was free New Year's Eve. We would explain that we had this really great wedding party for him, and wanted to book him. And we wouldn't take no for an answer.

Not all of our stuff was at this height of sophistication. We might call a drugstore and ask if they had Prince Albert in a can. And then the inevitable punch line, "Well, let him out!"

This may have been stupid, but Bart Simpson has brought the fine art of the telephone gag back to life each week, and a lot of people think it's brilliant!

EIGHT

LAST DAYS

WE WERE always politically aware. World events some-how had their due hearings on The Corner, all in good time. We had opinions on everything, although the "other side" was seldom heard from. We were ardent liberals, we agreed with each other, and the agreement made it all seem so right.

We were a neighborhood that booed Thomas Dewey when his picture went up on the newsreel screen. We thought the Rosenbergs were getting a bad deal, because, whatever it was they may have passed to the Russians oc-curred when we were allies. They had kids; they didn't deserve the electric chair.

Joe McCarthy was hated. Hated. No matter how naive our opinions might have been, we just knew that it was inher-ently wrong in the United States to tell on someone else. And as for the communists, about 30 percent of the country may have been communist during the height of the Depres-sion. I thought this hate of McCarthy was universal until I got a job where a lot of my co-workers supported him. It made me very uncomfortable, but it was also eerily fascinating to hear some right-wing opinions. Still, I loved it when Joe Welch destroyed the man during the Senate hearings.

I got to interview McCarthy near the end of his life, when I was doing my radio show in Miami. He wasn't such a bad guy then. I tended to think of him as caught up in the times, but then I reminded myself that he WAS the times. He had created this witch-hunt mentality which was such an embarrassment for the nation.

The Eisenhower-Stevenson election of 1952 really caught our attention. We were in our late teens and were passionately interested in this election. I had seen Dewey drive by in a car once, but Stevenson was the first presidential candidate I ever personally watched speak during a campaign rally. It was in Herald Square in Manhattan, and it was a rally arranged for by the International Ladies Garment Workers Union, to which my mother belonged. He was introduced by the union's president, David Dubinsky. To me, it was as big as seeing Bogart in person.

While Stevenson had seemed to be a reserved, thoughtful man, the rally was loud and passionate, and I felt swept up by the campaign frenzy. I loved the clipped tones of Stevenson's voice. I liked his name; it had bearing. I liked his manner and his presence, and I loved the homilies he delivered in his speeches. And his liberal message hit home with me. He seemed born for the presidency, whereas Ike was a war hero, not even affiliated with a political party when he was asked to run.

I had Stevenson on as a radio guest years later. I said on air, "I've never said this to a guest, but I've admired you all my life."

He replied, "You have the quickest appraisal of greatness I have ever seen in a host."

The newspapers influenced our thinking a great deal, and none more so than the bastion of liberalism, the New York *Post*. The *Post* had columnist James Wechsler, and they supported Governor Herbert Lehman, whom we liked because he was Jewish and liberal, and, to our thinking, he did good things.

With so many papers in town, you were at least offered a wide range of opinion. Today's kids don't have that diversity. You really have to search hard for it. There are fewer papers, and even with the proliferation of "thinking" television programs, kids don't seem as interested as we would have been. That's one reason I feel especially good when a young person recognizes me and tells me he watches or listens to my programs.

The tabloids were popular with us because they could be so easily read on the subways, which were our familiar mode of transportation. Sure the *Times* had good writing and bureaus all over the place, but it was full-size and hard to hold, and all of their stories were continued inside, so it was pretty much unmanageable while standing on the subways. The *Mirror* was, as the name implied, a mirror image of the *Daily News*. I always had a problem with the newsprint of the *Mirror,* and people would laugh about my rantings about the smudges you'd get from the *Mirror* that you wouldn't get from other papers.

We read the *Daily Worker,* the communist paper, because it was interesting to see how they would put a sociological slant on sports news. The diversity of papers was terrific. By the end of a day we would have read them all, and then we'd go out after dinner and see the pink night owl edition of the *News* with the early ball scores and the *next day's* headlines, and we thought — you can't improve on this!

Sam Maltz once chased me for two blocks with a crowbar over my newspaper-reading habits. He would use the crowbar to hold down his newspapers from the wind. Each day I would come by, slide the crowbar aside, and read each paper, cover to cover, then put it back. No harm done; I was very neat about it. Sam would complain, but I'd say, "What are you worried about? That the papers will wear out?"

One day I miscalculated the wind conditions, and when I forgot to replace the crowbar, all the papers blew apart and flew into the street. Sam came storming out of the candy store, grabbed the crowbar, and for a moment, didn't know whether to go after his papers or me. He chose me and we had a run down the street under the el which was the on-foot equivalent of Gene Hackman's car chase in *The French Connection.*

Mel Berger was our basketball coach at the J, and he was one of the first to go to Korea when the war, or "police action," began. His departure opened the way for me to become the coach, and thus I am the last basketball coach the Warriors ever had. We played in two leagues, including being the only Jewish team in the YMCA league. We finished second, a very proud accomplishment for a rookie coach.

There was no formal end to the Warriors. In fact, technically speaking, they still exist today, certainly in each of our hearts. But one by one, Warriors were leaving the neighborhood. Some were getting married, some were going into the army, some were taking jobs in the city that left them little time for the clubroom. Unlike a lodge or a fraternity, this was never intended to be a club that brought in new young members. We were just a bunch of friends together to the end. And the end was approaching.

My mother wound up with my Warriors jacket and still

had it when she moved to Miami, but it eventually vanished into that black hole in the universe where all boyhood treasures go. Like Puff the Magic Dragon.

Herbie went into the Army and found himself stationed in West Germany, which was not exactly the front lines during the Korean conflict. In fact, he wound up coaching an Army basketball team, and finished second to a team on which Larry Costello, later an NBA star, played.

In 1951, I was classified 3A by the Selective Service because I was supporting my mother. But as the war heated up, I was moved up to 1A, particularly since my mother was working. I wasn't especially fond of the war, but unlike the Vietnam era, this was something we did without much fuss. Herbie had gone, and now it was my turn. There was patriotism in my past. My father, FDR, Auntie Bella, the great heroes of World War II. It was okay.

In November of 1952, I got my letter of "greetings" from the United States of America. I was to report to the point of embarkation, 33 Whitehall Street, to begin my distinguished military service.

I got a crew cut before I left, thinking I'd rather have it done myself than by military barbers. And we had a big party, with all my friends, and my mom, who was in tears. She hugged me in front of everyone saying, "My boy, My boy," and there was sadness and happiness in the room. "How proud your father would be to see you serving your country."

She wanted to go with me to Whitehall Street, but I wanted to do this myself. I was nineteen. So on a cold, dark November morning, she went to work, Marty went to school, and I took my duffel bag, got on the el, and headed for Whitehall Street.

"Good morning, gentlemen," said the greeting officer

when he had us all lined up. "Under a new concept inaugurated by Selective Service, half of you are going into the United States Navy. The Navy feels it has not been getting enough enlistments. Thus, during the next three months, half of you will be going into the Army, and half of you will be going into the Navy. Those of you with blue folders will be going into the Navy."

I looked down. It was blue.

A Jewish kid in the Navy? I couldn't even swim. I didn't like the ocean; I didn't like swimming pools. We have a swimming pool where I live today; I've never been in it.

I wasn't going to be at Fort Dix, in New Jersey. I wasn't going to be able to visit Brooklyn on leave. This wasn't in my plans.

We were scheduled for our physicals. I had found a friend, a guy from the neighborhood, Georgie Berkowitz. We would go for our physicals together.

"Those of you who wear glasses, you'll go last so you won't hold up the line," they announced. I dropped back.

Now I was going from one checkup station to another. And I'm buzzing through. Pass, pass, pass, pass, pass, pass, pass. Now came the eye exam.

"Take off your glasses, Zeiger."

I couldn't read the chart. But that was okay, as long as I could read it with the glasses.

Only one step left now, the swearing in. We moved to the next room.

Suddenly, a voice bellows, "ZEIGER?"

"Yes?"

"Come here a minute."

I stepped forward. An imposing-looking officer stared at me.

"Mr. Zeiger, go home."

"Home?"

"Yes, home. You are being reclassified 4F. Our eye requirements have changed. You now exceed the limit of vision in one eye. We cannot require contact lenses."

Contact lenses were in their infancy. Today, you could be accepted with them. Back then, only glasses were considered for induction. And if your glasses fell off during combat, and you were helpless without them, you could lose the war for the USA. If contact lenses were permitted, I would have been accepted.

For a moment I was relieved. I had observed how the tone of the officers changed once the guys had passed and were sworn in. No more Mr. Nice Guy. "ALL RIGHT, GET IN LINE, ON THE BUS, MOVE IT, MOVE IT, MOVE IT."

And off went the bus. And I'm standing on the street with my duffel bag. The only one.

I am embarrassed as hell to go home. Some war hero. Some party. I got on the subway and headed back home.

My brother was still in school, my mother still at work. I decided to go to 86th Street, to the shop where my mother was sewing. It was 11:30 in the morning. It wasn't even lunchtime yet.

I walked in, and our eyes met.

"Lawrence? You didn't run away, Label, did you?"

"No, Ma, I was rejected. Bad eyesight."

And all over the streets of Bensonhurst, word spread. "Larry ran away, Larry ran away!" Hoo-ha came by and was the first to tell me that he wanted the wallet back that he'd given me at the party.

Larry the war hero.

College was not yet something that every good student aspired to. As children of the Depression, we knew that it was acceptable to go to work after high school to help your family. But times were changing, and more people were thinking of college. Herbie's sister had gone to Brooklyn College, and Herbie himself had made up his mind to go to City College in Manhattan, just to be different. I never gave much thought to this. My grades were low, my heart was on radio broadcasting, and my mother needed the money. I went to work for UPS after high school, got rejected by the Navy, then wound up delivering Borden's milk. It was safe to say that I was at loose ends.

Four years later, Herbie was due back from Germany. I was twenty-three. He did not feel like a war hero, of course, and he wanted absolutely no fuss over his return. He went so far as to inform his parents that he would be arriving on September 6 at such and such a place, on such and such a boat.

With idle time on my hands, I double-checked Herbie's orders, and discovered that he would in fact be arriving on June 20, on a different boat and at a different landing site.

Herbie may not have seen action, but he had an interesting military career. He was assigned to an outfit that guarded the east-west border in Germany at the height of the cold war. It was the 14th Armored Tank Division, one of the first to patrol post–World War II borders. Herbie felt out of his element with a lot of southerners in his troop, guys saying, "Ahm gonna kill me a commie today." He wanted to come home and resume his life quietly. They were not "the best years of his life."

But when he landed, I was there with his parents, with Joe Bush, another Warrior, and with Hoo-ha, awaiting his arrival. It was smoother than Hoo-ha's return of a few months earlier.

Hoo-ha's boat had docked. The procedure was, the of-

ficer would call off a name, and the person would disem-
bark.

"Harper, Private Gary."

He'd leave the boat.

"Hemund, Private Robert."

He'd leave the boat.

"Hightower, Private John."

He'd leave the boat. The procedure worked beautifully,
and was a study in military precision. There could be no
doubt that we were a superior military force.

"Horowitz, Private Bernard."

This was Hoo-ha. We heard his voice.

"What do you want?"

He hadn't been paying attention.

There were embraces all around. Herbie didn't want to be
met, but now that he was, he felt terrific. We all walked
slowly away from the boat. At one point the two of us were
together. "Larry, you look great. Nothing's changed."

"You're right, Herbie. We're still Spark and Plug, together
again."

"Still working at the dairy?"

"Yeah, still selling Borden's milk. It's going well."

"How's your mother? How's your brother?"

"Fine, fine."

There was a silence of a moment or two.

"Herbie, I got married."

"You got married? Who'd you marry?"

"A girl named Frada. We have an apartment in Sunnyside."

"Do I know her?"

"I don't think so. Maybe you met her once."

"What made you get married, Larry?"

I wasn't sure I knew the answer. I knew it had been a cold winter. I knew that my friends had gone off to war, or off to work, or off to college, and that I was lonely. I would go to The Corner and no one would be there. Or younger kids would be there.

Frada Miller was a nice girl, plain, no makeup, nice. I knew her through her cousin Julie, who had married a friend of mine. I don't remember that we ever had feelings for each other, but she must have felt a loneliness, too. We had a wedding ceremony. Marty was my best man. We had a reception in a catering hall. We had a honeymoon in Miami Beach, the first time I ever flew in a plane, the first time I ever went to Florida.

We had a white couch in our Queens apartment that was our best piece of furniture. She loved that couch.

I didn't always go home at night. If I had hooked up with an old friend from the neighborhood, I might just stay over in Bensonhurst and sleep in my old bed. I guess I just wasn't ready to take marriage all that seriously. I had gone to Sam Steinberg's wedding. When the Rabbi said to his bride, "Take Sam's hand and never let it go," I blurted out, "You gonna take her to work with you, Sam?" It is safe to say that I wasn't quite ready for marriage.

One evening I brought Hoo-ha home for dinner. It was getting late and Hoo-ha said, "Well, I suppose it's time to go."

But I said, "No, no, you can stay here tonight."

Frada wasn't especially happy about this, because the only place he could sleep was on that cherished white couch, and he would certainly make a mess of it with his Wildroot Hair Tonic.

So, after some discussion, we wound up all sleeping in the double bed. I was in the middle. Frada was on my right.

Hoo-ha was on my left. At 5:00 A.M., I had to wake up and go to work delivering milk. And I left the two of them sleeping in the bed together, with the space in the middle where I had been. I didn't give it a second thought.

I had always been a voyeur for radio stars. In the mid-fifties I would stand in front of CBS in the hope of seeing Godfrey. I would stand in front of WNEW radio and hope to meet what I considered to be celebrities. Marty Glickman was the only one I ever met. "Hiya, Marty, I'm Larry Zeiger from Brooklyn, and someday I'd like to be a radio announcer."

"Stick with it, kid, you can do it," he said to me.

James Sirmons was the chief staff announcer at CBS. To me, he was a big celebrity. He was the voice that would say, "*This* is the CBS Radio Network." Or he might say, "Stay tuned for . . . 'The Shadow.'"

I saw him on the street one day — who would recognize this man except me — and I told him that I'd really like to get into radio. Did he have any suggestions?

"Try Miami," he said. "It's a big, growing market, there are no unions, they have big stations, small stations, guys on the way up, guys on the way down, a lot of good people to meet, a lot of opportunities."

And so there came a day in 1957, when I was twenty-three, that I got on a bus and headed for Miami. The Dodgers were in their final weeks in Brooklyn. The Warriors were only a memory. My brother was off at college. We were grown men. Brooklyn was still wonderful, but it no longer seemed able to provide us with the answers to our dreams. Those dreams were greater than our parents' dreams had been. My father's dream was the sea breeze you would get in Bensonhurst. He didn't live to feel it, but his family did. Now it was time for me to chase my dreams.

I said good-bye to Frada. It just hadn't worked out. The marriage was brief and came of loneliness, but it didn't answer the loneliness.

I said good-bye to my mother. I would be staying with my Uncle Jack, her sister Rose's husband, in Miami. I would keep in touch and let her know when I got a job.

I said good-bye to Herbie and Hoo-ha and Ben the Worrior, who couldn't believe I could leave the dairy business without any job prospects lined up.

I found a job at a small AM station, WAHR, which I fell in love with because they re-created Brooklyn Dodger games. Marshall Simmonds, the general manager, hired me as a morning disc jockey. He told me that Larry Zeiger wasn't a show-business name, and he suggested King.

And so before long, I called home and told my mother that I was now Larry King, and I was on the radio.

And she told me not to catch a chill in the cool night air.

NINE

THE RETURN

Couple of years ago I went to see the house on Avalon. It was gone — not just the house, but the whole neighborhood!

I went to see the ballroom where me and my brother used to play — the whole place, gone.

Not just that, but the grocery store where we used to shop, gone . . . all gone . . . gone, ahhhh . . .

I went to see where Eva lived, off Poplar Street. It isn't there, not even the street, it isn't there, not even the street!

And then I went to see the nightclub I used to have, and thank God, it was there! Because for a minute, I thought I never was.

— Sam, final scene,
Barry Levinson's *Avalon*

I DIDN'T KNOW whether the sight of my childhood haunts would grab me by the heart and bring tears to my eyes, nor had I given it a lot of thought until this project came along.

But yet, when I felt the emotional calling of the sidewalks and playgrounds of decades past, I knew that somehow, those memories were deep, and awaiting this moment. Whether Brooklyn would reveal herself to me as a childhood in ruin, a painfully sad jolt, or as a spiritually uplifting embrace of my roots, I couldn't predict. But this assignment required a return, a capping of the total experience. I needed once more to smell this county, to witness its hurried frenzy, to take myself back to the buildings and trees and blocks which would surely be much smaller than I recalled.

Yes, there was trepidation heavily mixed with the anticipation, and the rainy summer day we selected in the summer of '91 was cast upon us as though forcing melancholy out of me.

I decided against using a limo to go out there, even though the car service I use in New York always provides me with one. "A plain sedan might be better," I told them. "We don't want to attract too much attention." We headed over the Brooklyn Bridge and deep into the Borough. Brooklyn is not a tourist spot. There is not a single functioning hotel, I was told. The St. George, where Dodger players stayed, where visiting teams stayed, and which claimed the "world's largest indoor saltwater pool," was now an AIDS hospice.

We passed pockets of nicely maintained residential communities, and retail streets without the recognizable names of national boutiques. There were no Benettons, no Victoria's Secrets, no Brentanos, no Laura Ashleys. We saw a lot of mom-and-pop clothing retailers, pizza parlors, taverns, and "French dry cleaning." Some neighborhoods seemed so forgotten that even Pepsi-Cola had abandoned them. On a wall we saw a small billboard reading "Say Pepsi, Please," a slogan which might be thirty years old.

"Lenny," I asked my driver, "what do they call this neighborhood we're in now?"

"Death," he replied with a laugh. I told him he had made the book.

There wasn't a lot of traffic out. It was a rainy Saturday morning, and there were few people visible in a borough whose population is larger than Philadelphia's. It was about ten in the morning. I wondered where they were.

Suddenly, in trying to make a left turn, we were cut off by — of all things — a stretch limo. Someone had more guts than we did.

"That's Barbra Streisand," I joked. "She's doing a book, too."

I thought of the saloon as we drove. Somehow, I was more focused on the saloon, at 1925 Fulton Street, than on my home on Howard. Every time Sinatra sang "like fine old kegs," in "It Was a Very Good Year," I had the image of dad's "store," as he called it. I'd work the tap, *feel* the neighborhood more. It was the place where the cops hung out, where I was made a junior police officer.

The rain was pelting the car harder now as we got nearer. I could feel the direction as though I were a compass, while Lenny fumbled with a street atlas.

Herkimer Street — we played here. I hung out on Herkimer a lot. "Make a left somewhere around here, Lenny. We're gonna hit Howard."

Fulton was to the left. I felt that, too. And suddenly, there was Fulton Street, not the Fulton Street of Manhattan, with the fish market, but our own Fulton Street, the one that had Eddie's saloon on it.

Atlantic Avenue was to the right. There used to be a trolley line on it. The tracks were gone, but the Long Island Railroad ran overhead, the salvation of suburbanites who moved from Brooklyn and Queens and were able to commute to their city jobs by whooshing past their old neighborhoods. Was the LIRR there fifty-five years ago? Probably not, I thought.

Howard Avenue was eluding us. I knew we had it surrounded, but a detour on Fulton, where they were digging up the sewers, turned us around. We can't think of sewers without thinking of Art Carney's Ed Norton character in "The Honeymooners," can we? And sure enough, as the streets rattle past, there's Ralph Avenue — a coincidence for Mr. Kramden's benefit? — and Chauncey Street, the fictional home of the Kramdens and the Nortons. Gleason called the neighborhood Bensonhurst on the program, which, of course, it wasn't. He knew better. But he must have done it intentionally, knowing Bensonhurst somehow sounded funnier, and he would get more laughs with it over the run of the show. Like a comic writer who knows when cheeseburger is funnier than hamburger, Gleason had the touch. He was right, of course. Bensonhurst does *sound* funnier than East New York.

The trees, I remembered. I think *A Tree Grows in Brooklyn* was set around here. People don't expect trees in Brooklyn, but there are four or five on most blocks, scrawny, and unimpressive, but sticking there between the curb and the sidewalk, pretending to enjoy their surroundings. A tree in East New York was like a nun working the subways to raise money for Catholic Charities. There are better assignments, but everybody does what they're told. This was my world.

Howard Avenue. We'd hit it. We had to find 208. This was a bad area now. I *felt* that 208 was going to show up on my left. And I *felt* almost a magnetic pull that way — up more. There's 224. It's written in crayon over the door. Sumpter Avenue. That was my corner.

"That's it, Lenny. Pull over behind that red car." For a moment, I hesitated. I felt just a little frightened to get out of the protection the car offered. But then, why had I come here this day? I opened the door, jumped out, crossed the small street, and looked longingly at the two-story structure. My God, it was exactly as I remembered it. Smaller perhaps, than my childhood memory had photographed it, but it was 208 all right. The fence that I had fallen from and broken my arm was still there. The stoop on which I had sat when the man with the comic books drove up — still there. I took a deep breath. It had been forty-six years since I had stood on this very pavement. It was raining hard now, but it didn't matter. I was nine years old again.

I drank in another long look. Then we spun around the block. I had to find the saloon. While I was somehow sure that 208 Howard was still there, I didn't have the same feeling about 1925 Fulton. I expected it would be gone.

I knew it was only a few steps away. It was around the corner from Howard, but my bearings were turned around for the moment. We saw a postal worker wheeling her cart of Saturday deliveries. I got out and approached her, and asked her about 1925.

"Well, the post office is 1915," she said, "so it must have been right around — there." She pointed to an unnumbered, boarded-up row of ground-level storefronts. There was a four-story apartment building atop them. It was hard to tell whether the apartments were abandoned or not. But yes, that had to be where Eddie's was.

I didn't look at it with the certainty I had looked at the existing structure at 208 Howard. Yes, there was no doubt that dad's "store" had been right there. But it was eerie to see it boarded up. Almost like seeing a grave site. I knew that was the spot. The postal worker had confirmed it, but I knew.

"Drive down Howard once more," I said to Lenny. We paused again in front of 208. It took me forty-six years to return here. I couldn't imagine ever coming back again. What for? Maybe to show a grandchild? Perhaps, but I'd be in my seventies before one could appreciate it. This might be my last look.

We rolled slowly down Howard, past Bainbridge, Decatur, MacDonough, and Macon. I knew where we were going. Saratoga Park. Right there on the right. That wonderful, floral smell on spring evenings. Sometimes I smell it, but only in the northeast. Never had it in Miami, never in Washington. I don't know what it was, but it stayed with me.

Saratoga Park. Where dad and I would go for a Good Humor, provided I kept my end of the deal and didn't tell my mother. It might spoil my dinner. This was our place. Of everything I'd seen so far, this was the most special. For it belonged only to Eddie Zeiger and Larry Zeiger. My mother wasn't part of this and Marty wasn't part of this. It was our secret park.

I didn't want to stop; I didn't want to get out; I didn't want to walk in the park or take a photograph. It would have been too much. This is the place where I would have lost it. I would have cried.

"Drive slowly past this park," was all I could say to Lenny. I had a knot in my throat. I looked at it through the car window with the rain falling. I didn't even open the window to see if the smell was there. This part was too emotional.

"Okay," I said. "Let's go."

The drive was a long one. We went through Flatbush, the name most associated with the Dodgers, and past the Prospect Park subway station, which was the stop for Ebbets Field. I didn't even bother to look to my left as we went by the street that would have taken me there. Ebbets Field came down with a wrecking ball in 1960. They had the gall to paint the wrecking ball like a baseball, as though there was something funny about it.

We had taken the subway to Coney Island as kids, but our drive to Bensonhurst on moving day had been the first time we had ever made the trip to the "other end" of Brooklyn by car and moving van. It was a long trip, punctuated by very frequent red lights. Even now, with the greater patience of an adult, I could see what a journey it had been. Simply because we still had a Brooklyn address did not mean this was no big deal. It was another world, a new life. I must have realized even then that I would never see the old neighborhood again.

Ocean Avenue! Boy, it looked great. Very clean, too. It reminded me of long walks on Yom Kippur, dressed in our best. We'd walk miles on the Avenue, or on Ocean Parkway. This neighborhood would have been a dream to us. Ditmas Avenue! You had to know the super to get one of those apartments, and you still had to pay $125 a month.

"You gonna cut over at Avenue J?" I asked Lenny. "This would have been the way we came in forty-six years ago," I said. Avenue J would take us to Bay Parkway, our main street.

Ah, Bay Parkway. It's Congressman Steven Solarz's district. I always tell him it was my neighborhood when I have him on a program. We drove past the Marboro Theater, which was now four movies in one. Over there now, on the right, stood the Jewish Community House. The J. The site of so many precious moments. It was the center of our world. It felt good to see it still standing, still providing pleasure.

"Make a right on eighty-second, Lenny," I said. In a minute, we made another turn onto 83rd Street, my street. On the right, with a big American flag flopping out the middle window, was 2133. The point of arrival in 1944. The start of a new life. Flags had been everywhere in '44. In the days following the Persian Gulf War, they were again proudly on display. This remarkable journey home was now met by the remarkable coincidence of a new patriotic fervor at work. After so many years in which the display of the flag had become a political statement, not a matter of national pride, I had returned just in time to find it back in its classic place in America. The flag in 1944 had forty-eight stars; otherwise, it was as though I had been there yesterday.

We had no trouble parking right in front. It still seemed like an easy street to find a space. There were fewer trees than I remembered, but the street looked terrific. It was mostly Italian now. I could sense that the whole neighborhood was Italian, although you would see some signs in Russian here and there to accommodate the fifteen thousand Russian Jews who had arrived in recent years.

Our home now had an attractive yellow siding. The gate and fence were still there, painted a handsome red. The driveway had been paved and care had been taken to keep the place in top condition. Over the driveway hung a harvest of green grapes on a metal structure of supporting poles. In the back, past a small child's swimming pool with floating inflatable dolphins, was a well-kept tomato garden. I went to the front door to ring a bell. All three buzzers said "Marra," indicating one family had the whole place.

An Italian gentleman in his forties came around from the side to see what we wanted. I introduced myself to him. Brooklyn, having very little cable television, was not an area that would know much about CNN or Larry King. But he knew. A cousin of his, he explained, had once heard me on the radio mentioning my old address and had announced her new, indirect celebrity status to the whole family. Her cousin lived in the house once resided in by Larry King of

Mutual Radio. The Marras had bought this place from Sal Licari, our old landlord. A direct link! Mr. Marra smiled broadly when we mentioned the name.

This Mr. Marra did not seem one to be overly impressed by the presence of a media person, but he was gracious and pleased with the compliments we were bestowing on the condition of the house. It seemed that he had personally handled the alterations, or supervised them. A porch on the first floor had been closed off and made into a room. The front walk had been reshaped. And the rooms upstairs, where we had lived, he told us, had been rearranged, so that the bedroom and the kitchen were no longer where we left them.

Still, I was hoping for a chance to take a peek. The only view from outside that was satisfying was the view of the fire escape, outside our bedroom, where Marty and I had slept on stifling hot nights in the era before air conditioning. It was the fire escape on which I would sit and listen to Red Barber.

The upstairs Marras weren't home.

"I have to come back tomorrow," I said. "Could you tell them and see if I could visit around four-thirty?"

Off we drove to The Corner, Bay Parkway and 86th, by the train station. Again, the permanence of the place was heartening. The solid walls of the base of the stairs from the el were just as we had left them. The stairs down which I'd come after Bobby Thomson's homer to see that gloating creep Davy Fried. The stairs which I descended with my duffel bag after getting thrown out of the Navy.

There stood a man at Te-Amo Cigars on the corner, at the base of the steps. He was the proprietor. He was not the same one I remembered, but the way he stood, the way he stared, the way he went about his business, was exactly the way I remembered the nameless fellow who presided over that corner shop when I was a patron, purchasing halvah or cigarettes or a charlotte russe.

The Famous Restaurant — gone. The Feedbox — gone. The Davega appliance store, where we had watched the magical invention of television enter the store windows — gone. The clothing store where my brother had worked — gone. Maltz's candy store — gone.

But the look and the feel of the street was unchanged. I thought of the Benson Theater, where my mother would go on dish night and faithfully collect a full set. The day Hoo-ha's dream came true and he won a baseball mitt. There was activity, excitement. Each store carved out its little fortune for its owners without assistance from some big parent chain. Even Woolworth's was gone. It would demean the block to say it was a flea market, but none of the stores were high-priced boutiques. They all said "mom and pop" in appearance.

Suddenly, to my great surprise, I saw one that still existed from my youth. George Richland Clothing. Could it be? Same family?

What a great feeling. I went in. As I leaned on the glass counter and explained my mission, I was greeted warmly by George's family. They now ran the business. George himself had died just a year before at seventy-nine. We talked about George, how he had presided over this store which had outfitted all the Warriors and catered to our needs. Leaning on the glass counter brought back a flood of memories. I stayed almost half an hour. Although the place was busy, the Richlands reveled in talking with me. I made them feel good when I spoke so well of their father.

It was in front of Richland's that Herbie's father had told me, "Radio, schmadio, make something out of your life, stop with the dreams."

Four months later, I mentioned my visit to Richland's to someone.

"Richland's?" he said. "Didn't you hear? They closed it up. Didn't want to take a new lease. Happened a couple of months ago."

Just for the hell of it, I looked up their phone number and dialed.

"The number you have dialed, 372-1210, has been disconnected."

Keeping score? Richland's — gone.

For lunch, we stopped across the street at a kosher deli. It was 12:30 on a Saturday afternoon. We were the only customers. I had some kasha with my meal. Some Dr. Brown's cream soda. I didn't get the feeling that this was an acceptable order. Why was this a kosher deli? The waiters were Vietnamese, I think. There was clearly a major change in the ethnic structure of the neighborhood, although the Italians seemed to still have a strong hold on the place. But the Jewish population, once so important here, had gone, replaced only in recent times by the influx of Russian Jews, who probably required a major reacclimation to feel comfortable in this neighborhood.

I stopped into the Off-Track Betting parlor. It had been Sid's Pants. Had it been OTB when I was twenty-one, I would have spent a lot of time there; more than in Sid's. In my mind I heard the distant voice of a radio announcer giving us a call from the track. "... and now, from Jamaica. ..." I put a bet on a horse ridden by Julie Krone, and the horse finished fourth. It was a good thing there was no OTB around when I lived there.

But I got a good feeling from the OTB place. The first thing I had done after my heart surgery in 1987 had been to place a bet. It had been nine days after the surgery, a windy December day, and I felt so alive. No shortness of breath at all as I walked the city streets. I felt full of life and celebrated by marching into an OTB and placing a bet.

I bought a token and went up onto the Bay Parkway el platform. It looked down onto the street, with all its Saturday hustle and bustle, even on a nasty day. Under these tracks had been Gene Hackman's famous chase scene in *The French Connection*. A train arrived. It was modern and sleek, with a dull silver finish, graffiti-free. A far cry from the cane-backed seats and burnt orange cars that scooted us off in the forties and fifties.

Nineteen days after my visit, the body of a letter carrier was photographed being removed from the platform, his body riddled with four bullets. He was a retired city cop. I was shaken by the story. I had stood on the platform three weeks earlier and felt home, secure. But it was a fraud. It was not the serene comfort I had remembered after all. It was a changing environment. People were getting shot.

Bensonhurst Junior High School was next as we resumed the neighborhood tour. The sign over the door said Occupational Training Center. I could still sing all the lyrics of the school song. This was the famous school where the Moppo assembly had taken place. What? No bronze plaque outside to commemorate the event?

Eighty-fourth Street, between 20th and 21st. Major

punchball street. This was the block they'd close off for our games. I wonder how we got away with closing off the block?

Around the corner we came to Herbie's apartment building. Old women were sitting in front kibitzing. We followed the super into the lobby when he opened the door, and I was struck at once by the tile floor and the elevator doors. No change. The super looked at us suspiciously, and we announced our own departure.

A few houses down was Hoo-ha's house. In the alley on the right were the windows to our clubroom. I peered in, but saw nothing. Memories of the famous punch-out of Dora, of hearing her mother being rolled on the floor, of touching my first female breast, all came back to me. Wonderful things happened in the Warriors' clubroom.

On to Lafayette High! The setting for the "Welcome Back, Kotter" television series. A huge piece of real estate. Unchanged. The schoolyard, the front steps on which Iris Siegel had failed to accompany me, the majesty of the building itself, from which so many had graduated and gone on to success. The reunion on the occasion of the school's fiftieth anniversary had received national publicity a few years earlier. I could still sing Lafayette's song, too. Here was the building in which I'd almost leveled Judy Brickhouse.

Now it was on to the synagogue, an obligation I had fulfilled faithfully for the first year of my Bensonhurst life, saying Kaddish for my father, and when I approached thirteen, studying for my bar mitzvah with Rabbi Tarsis, attending Hebrew school every day. Both T'veret Torah, where I studied, and Sons of Israel, presided over by Rabbi Tannenbaum, had Russian signs in front. On the posting board in front of Sons of Israel, it said Rabbi

Emeritus: H. Tannenbaum. It had to be the same guy! Probably in his eighties!

We took some photos, and headed for the water.

The smell of the Atlantic Ocean told us we were arriving. Coney Island, however, was depressing. The famous structures that had made this New York's Disneyland for generations were standing in states of ruin. One park existed — Astroland — but it being a chilly, damp afternoon, we saw none of the rides spinning, even though there were ticket takers on duty. I thought I saw some tourists reading maps, but alas, they were Jehovah's Witnesses, standing dutifully by the el station to sell *Watchtower* magazines. A woman smoking a pipe walked by. The Parachute Jump, which I attempted once and once only, loomed in the background. The Cyclone, that world-famous roller coaster, which I also attempted once and only once, lay still. Nathan's — the original Nathan's — was open for business but not doing much of it. Other amusements were open but devoid of customers. The beach was deserted. What it must mean to these people to lose a Saturday afternoon in the summer to the bad weather!

I should make a note to tell Woody Allen that the milk bottles you have to knock over with a softball are still standing.

As the story went, there were these plaster-of-paris milk bottles in a carnival stand on the Boardwalk in Coney Island. The bottles, according to Woody, were designed to humiliate Brooklyn men. No matter how solidly you hit them with a baseball, they wouldn't fall. Cy Young couldn't have toppled them.

One fine day, the big hurricane hit, the biggest in a hundred years. The Hurricane of 1938. Trees fell. Power lines were cut. Cars were overturned. Even houses were downed.

Over on the Boardwalk, Coney Island was in ruins. Millions of dollars in damage. All except the milk bottles, of course, which stood perfectly still, awaiting the next sucker.

A few blocks over was Gravesend Bay, and the ball fields we used to play on with Sandy Koufax. They were muddied. The infield was all dirt. I could not imagine that they were in use. But it was my very own "field of dreams," and I needed a photo standing by my old position at second base. Off in the distance was the Verrazano Narrows Bridge, connecting Brooklyn to Staten Island. They had laid the cornerstone when I still lived here, but the bridge wasn't completed until I was in Miami. It was impressive for its length and its grace, the world's longest suspension bridge.

Being on the water, we could feel the unusual coolness of the July day. It was time to head back to the city.

The next day was more July-like. It was humid, sunny, and hot. I had been asked to speak at the J that evening, but I left early from Manhattan, with my brother Marty and his wife, Ellen, to return to the old neighborhood, and, hopefully, to find the third-floor Marras at home.

Marty, being four years younger than I, had lived through the same neighborhood, but had not shared my experiences. We didn't hang out together, except when we made him the Warrior mascot. He had his friends, I had mine, and our interests were not the same. He wasn't even a Dodger fan.

We were closer now than we had been as children. We could share one thing — we were roommates on the third floor on 83rd Street, and returning to that room would be a shared moment in time.

Although our gracious host of the day before, Mr. Marra,

had told his upstairs relatives that the famous Larry King would be back Sunday around 4:30, it must have left them unimpressed. No one was home. So we took some more photos outside and drove off for another look at Coney Island.

This time I had my wife, Julie, with me. She was like a kid seeing Disneyland for the first time. When we pointed out the original Nathan's she was awestruck. When she saw the Cyclone and the Parachute Jump, a hundred old newsreels and postcards must have flashed before her. We ordered a round of franks at Nathan's, walked up to the Boardwalk, and saw more life in the place than we had the day before. The weather had brought out the beach crowd, although there was plenty of space on the sand, and it was a far cry from the elbow-to-elbow crowds of hot Julys in the fifties.

The amusements were hopping, Astroland had passengers, and there was a happier feeling to the place. Before returning to the J, we stopped at a neighborhood Carvel for some yogurt. The owners recognized me; I introduced my wife and my companions, and it was like old times, chatting with the nice woman and her husband who ran the little corner store.

Back on 83rd Street, we were defeated. The third-floor Marras had not returned, and we couldn't see the old apartment. But as we had learned the day before, the rooms had been moved around, and our bedroom was no longer where it had been, and I suppose the visit would have been awkward, walking on these people's floors and seeing their personal effects. It was now their lives in that apartment, not ours.

Out on the street, two guys and a girl were tossing around a softball. I looked at Marty and said, "This coulda been us."

We walked over to the kids. They were really not kids,

but perhaps nineteen or twenty years old. Two had gone to Lafayette, one to New Utrecht High. They were friendly in a reserved way; they had heard of me, but they seemed to hold back a bit when I asked them about the neighborhood.

With smiles, they said it wasn't that good. It surprised me. It had looked the same, felt the same, smelled the same. I had assumed life was the same. But they said they were anxious to get out and move on. They said the old social/ athletic clubs were now street gangs. They said the murder of a black youth, Yusuf Hawkins, two years earlier had cast a pall on the neighborhood. It had happened only a few blocks away. Reverend Al Sharpton had marched through Bensonhurst and all the TV crews with their microwave trucks had been in the neighborhood for weeks. Whether that had changed things, I couldn't be sure. But these kids lacked the enthusiasm that we had felt. Their dreams seemed to be focused on "moving on." We had dreams, but they didn't begin with "getting outta here" because we hated the place. We loved Bensonhurst. Our dreams required territory that offered things we couldn't find at home. I wish I could have been a radio announcer in Bensonhurst. But my opportunity was elsewhere.

The J was still home. It was unchanged. The gym looked the same; even had the same clock on the wall. Photos in the hallway showed old championship teams. The one with Koufax seemed to gather the most attention.

About a hundred people had turned out to hear me that evening, which surprised me, as mimeographed invitations had been mailed only two weeks earlier. I spoke in a room I had never seen before. The J was the gym and the locker room to me, not these adult meeting areas.

It was my kind of crowd. A large woman with red hair kept interrupting my introductory remarks with corrections or footnotes. She was Brooklyn. A guy wanted to know where I stood on Canarsie. I didn't know there was a stand to be taken. I told him I supported Canarsie and heard it didn't smell anymore. He didn't like that I'd made light of some burning issue that was occupying Canarsie people at that moment, but we Brooklyn guys can give it back and forth to each other with the best of them.

Somebody brought a picture of me with our basketball team. I actually had a request to tell the Moppo story. I smiled, almost felt a tear in my eye, thanked him for asking, and told it. Twenty minutes later, having poured all my Brooklyn passion into the tale, making the characters come to life one more time, I took a sip of water, and put the program to rest.

The return had been complete. I saw almost everything I had wanted to see, experienced every kind of emotion I had ever known. Laughter, lots of it. Tears, mostly inside, but a few came out. In forty-eight hours I had relived twenty-one years — happy ones, sad ones, honorable ones, mischievous ones. I had heard Red Barber and seen the fire escape where I'd sat and dreamed of being a broadcaster. I had seen Saratoga Park.

To those who walk these streets each day, they are only so many slabs of concrete and steel and brick and mortar. To others, like myself, who had moved on, those inanimate objects were breathing that weekend, whispering memories to me, making my life full.

The beautiful thing about my years in Brooklyn was that it didn't take hindsight to appreciate it. We knew it was a great life while we were living it. Every day meant encounters with good people, shared experiences with a glowing optimism of the future. Did we have money? Nah. It didn't matter. We had friends and a sense of neighborhood and solid families and values, and if we got into mischief, it was harmless and we'd always live to see another day.

Hoo-ha became a Successful Manufacturer's Representative, and still talks the same. There's an ongoing debate over who does the best Hoo-ha imitation. He likes the fast lane, and I'm not sure who was a worse influence on whom.

Lenny Lefkowitz became the keeper of the faith. He was the last to leave Bensonhurst, moving to New Jersey in 1992. He knew where everybody was, and knew more stories about Layafette sports than anyone who ever lived.

Ben the Worrier is a singer named Bobby Benton, in Vail, Colorado.

Bucko became a cop in Connecticut. Inky became a dentist. Barry Rubin is a top entertainment lawyer in Hollywood.

Sandy Koufax found control and became the best baseball player of his era. He retired in 1966 at the top, went into the Hall of Fame his first year of eligibility, tried sportscasting for a couple of years, and has led a reclusive life ever since.

Naty Turner became a doctor, but died too young of cancer.

Arnie Perlmutter became a pension fund analyst.

Davy Fried bought a little bookstore in Long Island, and no doubt featured all the fortieth anniversary books about Bobby Thomson's homer in his window in 1991.

Iris Siegel married Asher Jagoda, now known as Asher Dan. They moved to California, divorced, and Asher married the actress Cara Williams. He's a major real estate figure there.

Toby Goodheart, where have you gone?

My brother Marty went to law school, married, had children, led a responsible professional life, divorced, married a wonderful girl named Ellen David, and is closer to me now than he ever was. We went through a long period when we were more or less out of touch. Now we talk every day.

My mother's sisters died in the order of their birth. All my uncles passed away too; even some cousins.

My mother moved to Florida some years after me, and basked in my growing celebrity. I would bring her with me to banquets and she had photos of herself with many of my guests. She developed cancer after a life without illness, a life of thirty-two years as a widow in which her children were her world. She passed away in 1976, and Herbie's mother, who lived in North Miami Beach, read the name Jennie Zeiger in the obituaries.

She went to the funeral and saw Marty and me, and I asked her about Herbie. We had lost touch. The occasion of the funeral had made me long for the innocence of my childhood, and I felt a need to contact him. By now, he had completed law school, married the lovely Ellen, had two children, and had become a successful author, lecturer, advisor to the Administration, and international traveler. A mensch.

Herbie and I picked up where we had left off, as though we were still Warriors, still carrying on the tradition of a neighborhood where we didn't know hate, only a love and a caring for each other, a sentimental throwback to a time that may not come again.

But, Herbie, there's still no way that Snuffy Stirnweiss could carry Jackie Robinson's jockstrap.

My daughter, Chaia, and my son, Andy, now adults, may one day walk with me and my grandchildren into Saratoga Park for some ice cream.

1–4–3, and Arrivederci!